IN THE
ONENESS
OF TIME

BY THE AUTHOR

The Toltec I Ching with Martha Ramirez-Oropeza

OTHER NONFICTION WORKS

I Ching Mathematics: The Science of Change

The Image and Number Treatise: The Oracle and the War on Fate

The Forest of Fire Pearls Oracle: The Medicine Warrior I Ching

I Ching Mathematics for the King Wen Version

*The Five Emanations: Aligning the Modern Mind with
    the Ancient Soul*

*The Spiritual Basis of Good Fortune: Retracing the Ancient Path
    of Personal Transformation*

Facing Light: Preparing for the Moment of Dying

The Soul of Power: Deconstructing the Art of War

POETRY

Palimpsest Flesh

Fragments of Anamnesia

IN THE
ONENESS
OF TIME

The Education of a Diviner

WILLIAM DOUGLAS HORDEN

3+4 :: 6+1 :: return

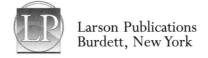
Larson Publications
Burdett, New York

ISBN-10: 1-936012-76-6
ISBN-13: 978-1-936012-76-3
eISBN: 978-1-936012-77-0

Library of Congress Control Number: 2015944831

Publisher's Cataloging-In-Publication Data
(Prepared by The Donohue Group, Inc.)

Horden, William Douglas.
    In the oneness of time : the education of a diviner / William Douglas Horden.
        pages : illustrations ; cm

    Issued also as an ebook.
    ISBN-13: 978-1-936012-76-3
    ISBN-10: 1-936012-76-6

    1. Horden, William Douglas--Education. 2. Divination. 3. Occultists--Education. 4. Intuition. 5. Consciousness. I. Title.

BF1773 .H67 2015
133.3   2015944831

Published by Larson Publications
4936 NYS Route 414
Burdett, New York 14818 USA
https://www.larsonpublications.com

24 23 22 21 20 19 18 17 16 15
10 9 8 7 6 5 4 3 2 1

TO ALL WITH WHOM I SHARE

A NAGUAL-PACT

CONTENTS

INTRODUCTION

My wife, Leonor, a devout Tibetan Buddhist, likes to say that I must have done something good in a past life to have met all the wonderful teachers I have had in this lifetime. Certainly, I do not feel I deserve the kindness or generosity of spirit that has been shown me by truly noble-hearted spirits. It is my hope that this brief record of the teachings I have encountered might repay in some small part the benevolence shared with me.

It was a different world when I was a young man. It was much easier to travel to remote destinations. There was not nearly so much information on spiritual traditions. And there were far fewer teachers. This latter point meant, on the one hand, that it was difficult to find any teachers at all, but, on the other hand, that there was a greater likelihood that their teachings were authentic.

When we were children in rural Ohio, I did not know anyone my age that did not practice water witching with forked sticks, usually of cherry wood. We dowsed constantly with our divining rods, imitating the actions of our elders seeking water to irrigate their crops. People who grew up on the land had, I think, a natural sense of the everyday mystical. It wasn't considered magical or supernatural—it was just one of the ordinary things you did hand-in-hand with the land.

The shamans I have met in Mexico are like this, too. One walks up to their adobe home and sits and waits for them to finish plowing the field or bringing firewood closer to the house. They are universally practical men and women who have been educated in the skills of reading spirit.

A Chan teacher was once asked, "What do you expect when you meet an enlightened teacher?" To which he replied, "I expect them not to be weird." To be a diviner is like this—to take the time to become sensitive to spirit and develop the skills whereby its intentions can be understood and, ultimately, communicated to others. It is not to be flamboyant or to seek attention. It is a sacred trust that ought be performed with an appropriate degree of humility as an act of service to the Whole. There is a second meaning to the story, however: for Chan teachers, the word normal referred to the inherent enlightened true mind, so expecting them not to be weird meant that they not demonstrate any traits of the artificial "abnormal" mind conditioned by social molding.

The education of a diviner, then, is not so much about learning a particular type of divination as it is about learning how to be fully and harmoniously integrated into the natural state of spirit.

The lessons I have recorded here all happened as I have recounted them. It is what some call a spiritual autobiography, a record of my inner initiations. Many of the spaces in between these critical events in my life have faded with the years, yet these moments remain perfectly clear, inscribed in the stone of my soul.

Now that this body is turning toward death, I find this act of reflection a fitting recapitulation of a lifetime spent in the company of great souls and, I trust, an intelligible testament to my undying gratitude for this world of spirit allies. I find, too, that in this backward gaze I see myself little changed from that boy water witching with his divining rod, constantly searching for the wellspring that lies hidden just beneath the surface of appearances.

PART ONE
TEACHINGS

*Please note that Part Two contains
a commentary for each of the
following chapters.*

PREAMBLE

2014

When I tell people I was born in a cemetery, they generally think I am speaking metaphorically.

"Weren't we all?" they often say, laughing, a hand going to my shoulder comradely.

This always surprises me. Of all the things I might call this world, the last to come to mind would be *a cemetery.*

ONE

1971

"No. No. No. You are trying too hard." Oddly, his disapproval didn't sting as much as soothe. Master Khigh Alx Dhiegh had perfect command of his voice.

"You have to concentrate in a way that opens the door to the Oracle so the other person might enter."

I opened my eyes, resolved to start again. Across the table, watching me with a combination of doe-eyed gentleness and falcon-eyed intent, sat the man who'd taken me under his wing nearly two years before. As with most our sessions, he wore one of the spectacular Chinese robes he kept in the closet of his office. A stick of incense smoldered nearby a flickering candle. Three antique coins lay on a silk cloth between them. Master Khigh's broad smile reflected an inner calm that only seemed to accentuate the mischievousness dancing in his eyes.

Without warning, he closed his eyes and began chanting a mantra under his breath. I did my best to match his breathing and let the syllables fall, pebble by pebble, to the bottom of my well. The air cleared, came into sharper focus, making it easier to make out the circle of diviners gathered in the marbled shade of an ancient pine. The lightest breeze bore the aroma of the sticks of incense from the center of the circle. Fleeting arrows of sunlight glanced off the coins lying in the lush grass. Papers shuffled, voices murmured, fingers pointed to this hexagram and that. Every sound echoed, amplified off the steep mountains enclosing the narrow valley. A gnat brushed my eyelashes, something scurried over my sandaled foot. One of the diviners looked up, noticed us, and waved us over to join the circle.

Master Khigh cleared his throat. My vision blurred as the air thickened again, concealing the scene behind the mist of the five senses.

"Enough for today," he said with gentle finality.

I'd learned better than to argue. But I shook my head resignedly as I stood up. "I still can't tell what it is that you're doing."

He beamed a perfect smile. It could mean anything: mocking me, empathizing with me, anticipating a cup of tea.

He leaned forward, whispering dramatically, "You have to learn how to make *the shift* on your own."

I nodded, taking it in. "Try harder without trying so hard, right?"

Master Khigh laughed appreciatively. "Now you're getting somewhere."

TWO
1974

"Someone's been teaching you how to *dream*," Dr. Sharp noted clinically, stressing the last word by drawing out its pronunciation. He tapped the spherical protrusion in the middle of his forehead with the middle finger of his right hand. He seemed to be staring at me but with a completely unfocused gaze, as if appraising the space around me. This was the kind of person I felt at home with.

Cocking his head to the right inquisitively, he asked with exaggerated politeness, "Who, may I ask, would that be?" The question seemed double-edged, half merely conversational and half oddly serious. This was our first meeting and I didn't want to give him the wrong impression.

I took my time answering. Averting my gaze, I took in my surroundings as I'd been taught, finding the right words by listening to the atmosphere of the place. His office was spartan, punctuated with various drawings and paintings that looked to be gifts from patients. A sturdy treatment table squatted in the middle of the room. Other than the desk and chairs where we sat, the only other piece of furniture was a strange knee-high contraption made of polished wood with leather padding. The room gave nothing away. It was part of his cloak of invisibility.

"I studied with a teacher for two years a little while ago but," and here I furrowed my brow to let him know I was taking his question seriously, "I don't recall him ever mentioning anything about how to dream. Have you heard of Master Dhiegh?"

Dr. Sharp leaned back in his chair, hands folded over his sternum. "Khigh Dhiegh? I thought he just taught the *I Ching*."

I shrugged, uncertain how to reply. A whole torrent of lessons wanted to pour out onto receptive ears but it felt like a childish impulse to defend my teacher's reputation.

He waited patiently for me to say something.

"He always said he was training me to be a diviner," I finally said.

"A diviner." He repeated it like he'd never heard the word before.

I nodded. "He liked to say that the only difference between people is their sensitivity to the One—and that diviners are those whose sensitivity has been heightened."

"Umm," he hummed pensively. "And he never mentioned that diviners were the first shamans?"

"Shamans," I repeated as if I'd never heard the word before.

"Call me Robert from now on," he said, picking up a pen and sliding a piece of scrap paper between us. "Have you ever heard of the *nagual*?"

THREE
1979

Someone had broken the ceremonial gourd.

"It has many years," Don Alfredo explained, turning it over and over, inspecting the crack that ran halfway down one side of the weathered gourd. "It belongs to my wife's father and belonged to his father before him."

He dipped the gourd in a pail of water and held it out at eye level. It bled like a mortal wound.

Don Alfredo shook his head sadly. "The *tesguineria* will never be the same without it."

I had an inkling of what he meant—I'd made many a toast, and been toasted by many, with that gourd. "Are you going to have to make a new one?"

He wagged a hand noncommittally. "First, we have to try to save this one." He stood and stepped indoors for tools.

I stood and stretched. The pine rounds we used for seats offered short-lived comfort. Turning to take in the mountains rising behind the house, I was struck once again by the timelessness of the scene. Don Alfredo's field of corn, beans, and chili butted up against the volcanic mountains that seemed to touch the sky. Winding out of the pine forests above, an arroyo cut the bottomland on its way to the Rio Batopilas that formed the other boundary of his ranchito. Standing there beneath the thatched roof outside the rock-and-adobe house, I inhaled one deep breath of tranquility after another.

It was the rainy season and it smelled green.

The afternoon storm had passed, trailing humidity out of the canyon lands below toward the continental divide above. The land had missed the rain, as Don Alfredo liked to say.

He returned with a small hammer, a very thin nail and a spool of fine copper "thread." By setting a piece of firewood vertically between his legs, he had a surface about the right size to hold the gourd. He started by delicately tapping a series of tiny holes all along both sides of the crack. It required painstaking attention to make sure he didn't create new cracks or split the existing one sideways. Once he had the holes in place—there were about twenty on each side of the crack—he began "sewing" with the copper thread. Beginning at the bottom, he ran the thread through the two holes on either side of the crack, tightening and knotting each pair with his teeth before going on to the next. From beginning to end, the whole operation took a couple hours—but the time seemed to pass in an eye blink, so immersed in concentration were we.

With the last knot wound tight, Don Alfredo dipped the gourd into the pail of water and held it out at eye level for a long moment. Not a drop leaked. Absolutely watertight.

He lifted it in a mock toast to me, took a long drink and passed it to me. I returned the toast and took a drink, mindful to examine the stitching carefully. I was aware that the value, the meaning, of the gourd had suddenly increased in a way difficult to put into words. Salvaging it from ruin, somehow, had made its sacredness more apparent. I raised the gourd to the sky as I'd seen him do ceremoniously and he nodded affectionately.

"There are no small things," I said, repeating one of the lessons he'd been drilling into me the past year.

His eyes darted over my shoulder and I turned to see his wife's brother, Melesio, running up to the house, grinning broadly. "Flash flood! Flash flood!" he called out excitedly, turning to race off to the arroyo before the surge could arrive from the runoff above.

I had seen Melesio, one of the great runners of the Tarahumara, run before but always in long distance races. I had never seen him sprint before.

He took five or six rapid steps, so short as to almost be running in place, and then, without an instant of time passed, he was about thirty yards away, sprinting toward the arroyo. Abruptly, he pulled up to a complete stop and looked back at Don Alfredo with a look of utter horror and guilt that was easy to read. I'd been adopted by the family, he'd forgotten I was from outside, he'd made a mistake, he'd revealed a secret. A big secret.

He must have received some signal from Don Alfredo behind me because he regained his composure, turned, and trotted off to the arroyo.

I stood like a doe in the headlights. A single thought slammed into the inside of my forehead, demanding attention: *He disappeared in front of me and reappeared instantly a hundred feet away!* But this was not the time to be sharp-eyed or sharp-witted. I needed to react wisely. There is much to be said for playing possum, sometimes.

I cast my eyes downwards, fixing my attention on the seam in the ceremonial gourd. Donning my most impassive demeanor, I turned back to Don Alfredo, giving every indication that I'd been completely absorbed studying the results of his labor the whole time.

He scanned my face without seeming to, glancing over its colors and contours the way he would of a patient coming for a remedy to some illness. He did not seem to find any sign for alarm there.

I held out the gourd with both hands, saying, "I am very afraid of breaking it."

He took it in his hands, running a thumb up and down the knots of copper wire, and, shaking his head decisively, replied, "I believe it is safe in your hands."

FOUR
1975

"Don't *wow* things."

Robert Sharp was teaching my wife, Leonor, some of his healing techniques.

"Your natural enthusiasm and kindness make you too quick to react empathetically. I don't care if someone comes to you and says, 'I was taken aboard a spaceship and they took me out of my body and stuck me in this one.' You can't make them feel like they're weird or abnormal. You have to act like, 'Oh, yeah, that's the second time I've heard that this week.' You have to make everything normal."

"Okay, I'll try," she replied as best she could face-down on the treatment table.

Robert looked up at me as he continued working on Leonor's shoulder.

"Remember. Don't *wow* things."

FIVE
1971

"Tell me, please, *where* exactly is the Oracle?" he asked.

I used Master Khigh's voice to help refocus my meditation, which had begun drifting away from the question. *Where, indeed, does the Oracle dwell?* How many times had I asked myself this in the past few weeks? I'd searched inside myself to no avail and convinced myself it did not exist as an object in the natural world like trees, mountains, rivers, wind or clouds. Yet I could contact it—or, rather, could open myself to being contacted by it—so it must exist *somewhere*.

The pursuit had become a kind of koan. It pulled at my attention, promising deeper communion with the Oracle if I could just break through the mental barrier. I marshaled my thoughts again, concentrating on *finding* the Oracle. But they scattered again right away. It all seemed as futile as blood running out onto sand.

"Perhaps, then, you could tell me what language the Oracle speaks?" His voice had a hint of mockery, as usual, but the words were obviously intended to act as a pointer. I followed them.

Symbols, I knew, made up the language of divination. As Master Khigh constantly reminded me, "An emperor asking about where to build the capital and a farmer asking when to plant the fields can obtain exactly the same hexagram and line changes, yet both their questions are answered perfectly. Such is the magical power of symbols." This I knew. Symbols formed the outer expression of the Oracle's *speaking*.

But what language is the Oracle *actually* speaking? What is it seeing? How is it describing what it perceives? I was surprised at the direction these new questions were taking me.

The trigrams of the *I Ching* spontaneously swam before my inner vision. But not in their usual three-lined forms. Instead, they appeared as *images* of their respective names—not as distant, self-contained "pictures" but, rather, as looming entities within the swirling landscape within which I suddenly found myself. Twilight was punctuated by lightning flashes, wind was howling, mountains rose at the edge of a deep abyss, the moon set into a bottomless lake, and I was a feather being blown haphazardly among titanic forces.

I gasped reflexively. My body jerked. My eyes snapped open.

Master Khigh sat in front of me with a broad smile.

"At last, at last," he exclaimed, clapping with one hand.

SIX
1969

"Your poetry says what I feel, I am very happy to make music with your words," said Moacir Santos, struggling to get the English out through his native Portuguese.

"Please," I replied, "it is my honor to be part of your work." One of the premier jazz composers of Brazil, he'd been called the "Alchemist of Jazz." We were meeting at his Spanish-style home in Southern California to discuss writing songs for a play.

His wife emerged from the kitchen with some fragrant tea and small cakes. We sat in comfortable chairs with an end table between us. Everything in the living room seemed superfluous, however, to the grand piano dominating the space.

He set his cup down abruptly and said, "When I read your words, I feel that you know Gurdjieff. Am I wrong?"

I was more than a little taken aback. I knew there was nothing in the lyrics he had read that could conceivably be read as influenced by Gurdjieff. It was an extraordinary insight. Or intuition. Or something else.

"I am only a student, of course," I replied. "But I admire his devotion to the mysterious."

Moacir moved to the piano. "You know his theory of octaves, then?"

I honestly felt as if I'd entered a dream. Here was one of the world's great musical artists inexplicably bringing up a subject that had completely absorbed me for months. It all seemed like the least likely of coincidences.

"That and the enneagram seem especially significant to me," I said, barely daring to jump into such a meaning-laden subject.

Moacir nodded, his hands settling on the keyboard. "And they are closely related, no?" A big full chord stretched out from the piano.

Before I could answer, he began playing scales with his left hand. "You remember how Gurdjieff teaches that the half tones in each scale form *shocks* that keep pushing transformation forward? You see, playing the scale with one hand, you cannot really *feel* that shock, it is more theoretical—but hear this, when I play different modes against each other—"

At that point, Moacir began playing scales in different modes with his right hand, pausing momentarily to accentuate certain confluences between the right- and left-hand scales.

"—now, we can feel the shock when we arrive at the half-tones in both modes at the same time—"

"What's that?" I asked, perplexed. "Is there a metallic taste in the air?"

"—which is magnified," he continued, dropping into a dirge-like composition, "when we disguise those intervals inside complex chord progressions—"

Slow and undulating, the piece fell into a recognizable cadence of rhythmic footfalls. The music of a sacred dance. I felt my heart slowing to fall into step with the song of remembering—for what else could it be called? It pulled up memories from the bottom of the bottomless pool of life, casting images onto the back of my eyes that were immediately recognizable but too intricate to grasp intellectually. Except that it became apparent that the music was turning backward, revolving back into the dark of time, unwinding all the complexities of the Many back into the essence of the One. As the music slowed, the images lasted longer, as if we were actually arriving somewhere closer to the center of gravity. Arriving somewhere we were coming to a stop.

Superimposed on the living room, as if its far wall extended out indefinitely, an entirely different kind of space opened up. A gigantic sphere of light pulsed slowly, throwing off infinitely smaller versions of itself, each of which traveled a different distance away before stopping and falling back into the sphere. The entire scene moved like a dance, like the very dance of creation, for the relationships between these lights possessed the same kind of instantaneous meaning one finds in dream images. It was *manifest* that each of these smaller lights was an individual being and that the distance each traveled away from the center was the *actual* distance from the act of creation—that each realized its own unique reflection of the sphere as the result of the diameter it established at the apogee of its travel. I was not aware of these relationships sinking into my awareness—it was all as self-evident as looking at a landscape in nature.

What struck me most was the difference in velocity between the small lights traveling away from the center and their return: the movement outward and away from the sphere seemed to be one of aching slowness, whereas the movement back inward and toward the sphere was nearly instantaneous. It reminded me of a ball snapped back on an elastic string. I was watching, I realized, the underlying reality of birth and death.

The music stopped.

The vision faded from view.

Only then did I realize tears were rolling down my cheeks. I wiped them away with a sleeve.

Moacir watched me with the most beatific smile.

"That's some shock," I said, barely holding back a belly laugh.

"I am very happy for you," he replied, standing and offering me his hand.

I took it in both of mine. "Everything has changed," I said gratefully.

He placed a hand on my shoulder, replying as if by rote, "And yet nothing has changed."

We walked to the front door in kindred silence.

"Don't worry, you will see it again," he said as I stepped out onto the porch.

I turned and raised my hand in salute.

"And now," he answered, closing the door softly, "back to work."

SEVEN

1971

"Now I know where I am."

Master Khigh Alx Dhiegh narrowed his eyes, looking hard at me. "Very well, tell me."

"I have been here before, I just didn't know how to get back." And I went into a detailed account of the experience I had had a year and a half earlier with Moacir Santos.

He listened intently, the tip of his index finger tapping lightly on pursed lips.

"This is certainly an unexpected sign," he murmured when I'd finished. "You had already seen the Oracle before we met."

As usual, his words threw me back on myself. I shook my head, trying to clear cobwebs.

"Now I'm lost again."

"Why? You were doing so well there!"

"I can see that the living images of the trigrams and the sphere of light are in the same *where*," I replied slowly. "But I'm more confused than ever trying to think of it as the Oracle."

He sat back in his chair and took a few minutes sipping his tea.

"Do you know why I dislike explaining things to you?" he finally asked.

"I have always assumed it is because you feel the best way to learn is by *doing*, by direct experience."

"So it is," he replied, nodding. "Nonetheless, rules are meant to be broken."

He made an exaggerated grimace and waved me to relax and lean back in my chair.

"The *where* you are learning to enter is the In-Between World. This is a very delicate matter and quite difficult to talk about without confusing the uninitiated." He set his teacup on the stand to his right, grudgingly warming up to speaking. "It is neither the world of matter nor the world of spirit. As you are finding out, it is quite real. An autonomous realm ordinarily hidden from the five senses. But quite real. It is the world of *pure psyche* that exists before it splits into conscious and unconscious, the first kind of awareness of *being* that exists before awareness of *thinking*. These living images you encounter are pure psyche itself before it is individuated into personal awareness. It is the World Soul that stands between the world of *spiritual intent* and the world of *animate manifestation*."

He paused, giving his words time to sink in.

"Think of it like water for a moment. In its more rarefied state, water is vapor. In its more solidified state, water is ice. The In-Between World is water-psyche. Soul. The realm of living images that translate the ether of spiritual intent into the ice of animate manifestation. This has long been called the realm of living archetypes, of *angels*. Not angels in the cute greeting card sense, you understand, but in the sense of *living messages* of the sacred. In the sense of archetypes emanating every individual form."

He cocked his head to one side, listening to what he was to say next.

"When I said you had already seen the Oracle before meeting me, I did not mean that the sphere of light you encountered was the Oracle. What I meant was that the *entire realm* within which it—and all the other living images dwell—is the Oracle. It is the World Soul and Its *speaking* in the symbolic language of images that is the Oracle. It is a place utterly familiar to infants and young children. It is the realm of awareness before words."

He took a sip of tea and, instead of returning it to its stand, held it between his hands.

"Gaining entry to this realm requires a peculiar kind of concentration," he said, staring into his cup as if it were a well. "It requires one-pointed concentration on a single focus, as if one were driving a wedge into empty space. This is the function of a diviner—to fashion a question of images, of symbols, and concentrate on those images to the exclusion of all else. But this is focused concentration devoid of words. The question needs to be fashioned of the same material as the Oracle itself. You have already seen that this can be accomplished through sacred music. We can say the same of sacred dance and art. But we cannot *think* our way into *being* with words. We have to revert to the kind of pure awareness we find in certain types of dreams that are filled with living symbols, the meanings of which evolve over time. Which is why the practice has been called realizing the dream body, or subtle body. By single-pointed concentration on their own pure psyche, diviners gain entry to the living dream substance of the In-Between Realm."

I decided to press my luck with a question. "When you say this realm is autonomous, you mean it isn't just in my imagination?"

He jerked his head up, coming out of his trance abruptly. "Precisely. It *isn't* in your imagination—your imagination is in it! That is what pure psyche is: Imagination! You are training your *imagination-body* to re-enter the universal autonomous imagination that has given it form."

"But—" I started to object.

He held up a hand, stopping me short. "You see? This is the difficulty we find in talking about this matter. You think you know what I mean by *imagination* before you have fully explored the question on your own."

He sat erect in his chair and signaled with his hand for me to do the same.

"Breathe," he said firmly.

"Focus," he said softly.

"And now, back to work," he said from a distance.

Which struck me as the least likely kind of coincidence.

EIGHT
1976

"I'm doing an article on the work of Dr. Robert Sharp and he gave me your name as someone who might talk about the technique he calls *the press*. Would you be willing to tell me what you got from the experience?"

"Of course," I answered the woman on the other end of the phone. "It trained me for the moment of dying."

NINE
1972

The Hotel Oasis was haunted.

Haunted by time, which had made its lower two floors uninhabitable. Haunted by the sea, whose salt air and occasional storms ate away at its every surface. Haunted by the jungle that edged up on it from every side, threatening to overrun its monolithic edifice and reclaim it as its own. Haunted, too, by the animals that were its only other occupants.

The night clerk led me up two flights of stairs to room 317 and wandered off whistling porpoise noises that receded back down the stairs, blending into the chirrups of the small brown bats feeding beneath the recessed lights of the balcony.

There were also the otherworldly croaks of the hundreds of geckos likewise feeding on the insects drawn to the only lights in a mile radius. They clung to the stucco walls and ceilings with their little round sucker feet, hanging just inside any shadow they could find, their bulbous black eyes too big for their heads, darting like arrows at every bug attracted to the lighted stucco. What led them to emit such eerie mechanical sounds was unclear. They seemed to come at random. They neither attracted nor repulsed other geckos. Nor anything else, for that matter. Perhaps they were just singing. Or chanting, maybe. It did actually sound a bit like Tibetan throat singing.

I stood there like that for a long time, letting the night pour over me. It was deep and wide.

And full.

But it was starless and moonless nonetheless: cooling moisture from the warm sea trapped against the mountains ringing the town condensed to cover the sky from prying eyes.

The ocean started and stalled like a dark idling engine. Like the *shhhuuuuhh* of the wind through high mountain pines, it was a prescient sound, the first oracle announcing the impending arrival—or return—of something momentous. Anxious and reassuring at the same time. Fragile and dangerous at once. The goddess perpetually ready to unite for the sake of love, that no tear shall ever go forgotten. The moon's consort. The world heart pounding in the world ear, pulse starting and stalling, dark idling engine driving the world hands into a frenzy of grasping. It echoed out there in the dark, as invisible as in the day.

An owl hooted from its roost in one of the palm trees erupting from the hotel courtyard. A few scattered floodlights illuminated the leafy fronds of the treetops that were eye-level with the third floor. Every room faced out onto the courtyard from a wide balcony that wrapped all the way around the horseshoe-shaped hotel.

It was there, next to the balcony's waist-high railing and beneath one of its recessed lights, that I settled into an armchair I had dragged from my room. Letting the haunting pour over me. It was deep and wide.

And long.

A profound and unbroken still held the hotel in thrall. Except for the otherworldly croaking of geckos. And the infrequent *huuuuu* of an owl. And the constant, nearly inaudible, heartbeat of the sea.

The night of time poured over me.

Lifetimes passed before my eyes.

Geckos darted from shadow to shadow.

The ocean dreamed.

Huuuuu

Geckos scrambled and swirled against the stucco like an Escher drawing.

I felt my electrons spinning faster and faster.

The ocean saw something momentous in its crystal ball.

Huuuuu

The geckos all froze stock still, pressing themselves into the stucco.

It is the sound of a few stray hairs on your worn cotton collar.

Involuntarily, I pressed myself into the armchair. Adrenaline kicked in and the persistence of vision gave way to the slow motion strobe effect of reality.

Snapshot of a wingtip just at the end of my nose. Snapshot of a wingspan stretching out in front of my eyes, to a distant wingtip on the far horizon. Snapshot of golden talons dangling like living daggers. Snapshot of feathers along wing, back, tail, rippling in flight. Snapshot of the biggest owl in all creation soaring past the tip of my nose like an archangel on a mission.

As fierce as any monster.

As close as your eyelashes.

As quiet as a forgotten ghost.

Over the waist-high railing it came, past my nose, crossing the balcony, straight toward the stucco wall outside my room.

Straight toward the wall, headfirst. Moving fast as a hungry owl.

At the last possible instant, however, it braked with wings and tail, suddenly turned vertical, facing the wall, and, in one fluid movement, plucked a gecko from the wall with its talons, turned in mid-air so its back was suddenly toward the wall, and began great slow gulping wing beats to pull its mass up and over the waist-high railing with its prize.

If it had gone by me the first time in slow motion, it went by this time in stop action. Click. Enormous cupped wings pulling air. Click. Enormous winged shadow carved into the tiles of the balcony. Click. Enormous golden talons clutching a gecko click, its lifeblood oozing click, its eyes' light flickering out click, its death rattle rising from my sacrum and spilling out my ears click, its last exhale a tiny puff of ivory mist. Click. Enormous obsidian raptor pupil reflecting me in this armchair click, sand-colored scimitar beak barely clearing the railing click, one last downthrust of wings brushes my face click, golden talons pulled up close into belly feathers click, silent ghost vaulting over the edge of the waist-high railing click, disappearing into the dark. Click. Dark. Click. Dark. Click. Silent ghost landing in the fronds of one of the palm trees lit by the floodlights below.

Click. Click. Click. Click. Click.

The afterimage of that obsidian raptor pupil pressed me deeper into the armchair.

TEN
1978

The cascade drummed against the water below. A pet deer, marked by the red kerchief round its neck, wandered among the pools carved into the volcanic riverbed. A red-tailed hawk circled between mountaintops above. A cobalt dragonfly rattled its wings as it patrolled its stretch of the river. Gentle sunlight lulled the breezeless day into a drowsy reverie.

"How do you see what your eyes cannot see?" Don Alfredo asked as he toyed with a round pebble he'd fished out of the pool beside us.

I trusted that this was a rhetorical question and so held my peace. Besides, the day was so perfect, I was having trouble marshaling my attention.

"There are two kinds of seeing," he answered himself. "The first kind, the normal kind, is *tame seeing*. It is a matter of letting the light come in through your eyes, of seeing what is already created, like taking in all this around us right now. The second kind, the rare kind, is *wild seeing*. It is a matter of casting the light out through your eyes, a matter of shining the new creation, of making the other world."

I must have looked like a dog cocking its head, hearing words but recognizing none of them.

"When the Europeans came, we said that they had cobwebs over their eyes because the ideas they already had made it impossible for them to see the world clearly. This is because their tame seeing was like trying to see through spider silk. But it was also because they had no wild seeing. Nothing could come out of them but what they already believed."

"They did not treat the Tarahumara well," I said sadly.

"They could not see we are human beings, too. They made us slaves to work in the mines they dug into our precious mountains. They had guns and were very cruel, so for a long time we suffered greatly in this world. That is why we strengthened our resolve to use wild seeing to create a new homeland in the other world. That is the world we live in much of the time, because it takes time to make the creation strong enough for everyone to occupy."

"Do I have cobwebs over my eyes, Don Alfredo?"

"Your vision is growing clearer all the time, Guillermo."

"Then why am I not seeing the other world of the Tarahumara yet?"

"You cannot depend on tame seeing for that. You must throw your vision out into the world where the soul roams free. Tell me, what does our paradise look like?"

I closed my eyes, trying to draw a picture from what I knew of the people of the *Barranca del Cobre*. "Herds of goats," I said, "grazing on the mountainsides. Wide fields of lush corn and beans and chili. Deep rivers full of trout and catfish. Many caves, enough for all the families to live in without having to build rock dwellings. Ceremonial clearings for rituals and games. Endless trails for running."

I opened my eyes. Everything was as before.

Don Alfredo smiled warmly, waving his arm at the valley before us with a sweeping motion. "Look, Guillermo, you have just described where we are. It has taken us a long time to bring the other world to life here in this world. We do not know how long we can sustain it in this modern world but this is what it will look like forever."

I felt as though my heart might break.

I saw where my spirit would forever return.

Nothing has changed, I thought, looking at the mountains and river and fields shining all around me.

And yet, everything has changed, my soul echoed.

ELEVEN
1973

"Do you want to go the long way or the short way?" asked our six-year-old Tarahumara guide.

"The long way," Leonor and I answered without hesitation. We'd already seen the access to the short way into the Copper Canyon: a climb down a sixty-foot limbed pine tree that had been lowered into place to serve as a ladder to a rock outcropping that led to a steep descent of rock climbing for several hundred feet. What lay beyond that on the way to the bottom of the 6,000 foot deep gorge is forever hidden from me behind the veil of common sense. Suffice it to say, if a Tarahumara ever asks whether you want to go the long way or the short way, take the long way unless you're part mountain goat.

We had stepped off the train at Divisadero and spent the first half-hour gasping at the immensity of the *Barranca del Cobre* spread out before—and below—us. The snaking Urique River has, over the ages, carved canyon after winding canyon between the towering volcanic cliffs. Leaning over the edge to see the river below was vertigo-inducing, amplified by the swallows jetting the updraft from the canyon floor and shooting past our heads like bullets. From the lookout point, the whole of the Copper Canyon seemed a vast plateau of ancient andesite—but a plateau cut into a thousand ribbons by the force of wind and water.

We approached a man sitting in the shade of the train station who was carving a violin out of pine and asked about the possibility of him guiding us to the bottom of the canyon. He looked us over, took in our backpacks, and asked how long we intended to stay down there. We replied that we only had enough time to stay a few days but would need a guide to help us with the return. He nodded thoughtfully, then replied that he had too much work to do to take several days off but that he would be happy to lend us his son, Jose, who could accompany us the entire journey.

I'm not sure what we were expecting but it certainly wasn't the boy of six who presented himself.

"Quira-va," he greeted us formally, extending his hand. To "shake hands" with the Tarahumara is to lightly press their fingertips between your thumb and fingertips as they do the same. I bent slightly to shake hands, amused at the boy's serious demeanor. Traveling through the Sierra, you get accustomed to people of all ages approaching and striking up conversations about the world "outside." Such, I assumed, was the interest of the young boy shaking my hand.

"Jose," he said clearly, touching his hand to his chest. He was dressed in the traditional white linen shirt and pants.

Only then did it dawn on us that here was our guide into one of the most rugged terrains on the continent.

"Guillermo," I replied, making the same gesture.

"Leonor," Leonor replied, making the same gesture.

"Do you want to go the long way or the short way?" he asked.

"The long way," we answered without hesitation.

"It is already late in the day, so we won't be able to arrive at the river until tomorrow. But there is a place to sleep," he reassured us, pointing at our backpacks, "about halfway down." Although his second language, his Spanish was quite good.

The trail was formed by thousands of years of footfalls on volcanic detritus. It was constantly being remade by rain and wind and footsteps. The persistent danger was twisting an ankle on the loose stone. The recurring danger was falling from the narrow path into the abyss of the canyon. Both these dangers were made more real by our backpacks and the way they could throw us off balance at unexpected times. On several occasions, it was necessary to jog across alluvial fans where the trail had been completely erased, leaning into the uphill slope and trying to ignore the sheer unbroken slope falling away downhill.

The long way, in other words, was challenge enough.

Jose walked along at what seemed a leisurely pace for him but we could not keep up, regardless of how hard we pressed. He would disappear around mountainsides and then sit and wait for us to catch up before taking off again. It took a little while for him to understand we needed to take the occasional breather—although it was still Spring in the Sierra, the sun was relentless and it grew hotter and more humid the deeper into the canyon we walked.

About a third of the way to the bottom, we came to a level platform of rock that jutted back into the mountainside. A narrow arroyo ran through it before dropping over the edge. Back against the mountainside stood a house of loosely-stacked stones.

"This is where I live," explained Jose. "Please rest here while I go say hello to my mother."

I appreciated his diplomacy. If we'd accompanied him to the house, his mother would have felt compelled to offer us food—an unnecessary hardship to place on the family. We took advantage of the rest stop to slip out of our backpacks and absorb the grandeur of the place. Walking to the edge of the precipice, we were awed by the sight of the Rio Urique far below and just how near the opposite wall of the *barranca* loomed. As much as anything else, however, we speculated about how wonderful such an upbringing would be for a child.

Jose returned shortly, carrying a cloth sling under one arm. He waited for us to don our equipment before stepping back onto the trail. The next few hours were at a more rapid pace, as the sun was relentlessly coasting westward, causing Jose to explain several times that it got dark quickly once the sun went behind the mountains.

The campsite was a level place alongside the trail, just big enough to pitch our tent. Jose watched intently while we set it up, walking around it several times as if making mental notes about its construction.

There was no firewood or kindling around, so we cooked over a backpacking stove, throwing all the ingredients into a pan over the single burner. As we began serving up the plates, Jose opened up the cloth sling and added a dozen tortillas to the dinner—"a gift from my mother," he explained. They were thick and fresh, almost a meal in themselves.

As the sun set behind us, the cliffs facing us swam in shifting hues, like oil on water, of reds, oranges, and magentas. It was like a fireworks show, over in just a few minutes, but it sent Jose scurrying off the trail like a hound on scent. He returned a few minutes later with an armful of dry tinder, mostly sage twigs, that he deposited in front of the tent. Removing a small box of waxed matches from inside his tunic, he carefully struck one, guarding it from the evening breeze, and set the brittle twigs afire.

Dusk descended on the Copper Canyon and all of a sudden, dozens of little fires sprouted up along the cliff walls. A drum sounded off in the distance, echoing off the opposite wall and then back again several times as it worked its way up the canyon. In response, another drum answered from across the *barranca*, its echoes spreading downriver. One by one, all the Tarahumara along the cliffs joined in with their own unique drumbeat, the canyon ringing with their echoes as each household bid Rayénari, the sun god, safe passage through the underworld.

Dusk gave way to dark and all the bright fires died away with the last echoes. The stars began to emerge like the campfires of the ancestors in the pitch of the wilderness night. You could touch the sky.

Jose rubbed out the last embers of the fire and excused himself, explaining that he was going to go home to sleep in his bed and would return early in the morning to continue our trek. We were reluctant to let a boy of six wander off in the night like that but his father had not asked us to watch out for Jose—he was our guide, after all, and we had to believe he knew what he was doing. Nonetheless, it was hard not to worry about him climbing all the way back up to his house in the dark.

Our concern for his safety was only heightened when we were awakened a couple hours later by the haunting screams of a mountain lion reflecting off the cliffs. After that, every nearby noise conjured up the vision of a cougar prowling just the other side of the flimsy tent. Eventually, though, the exertion of the day took its toll and we sank back into sleep.

Although we woke early, Jose was already sitting a respectful distance from the tent, waiting for us to rise. We cooked a quick breakfast, augmented again by some of his mother's handmade tortillas, and broke camp just as the sun cleared the facing cliff. The sky was clear turquoise, the sun was molten gold.

It was a long descent to the canyon floor. The nearer we approached, the sharper the descent until the trail unwound into a nearly vertical slide on water-worn stone to the river. Grateful to have finally arrived, we took a long break to remove our boots and soak in the cold clear current of the Rio Urique.

Jose had a place in mind for us to make camp, one his father had instructed him to take us to. It meant scrambling among rocks lining the river for another hour but, as we had arrived several hours before sunset, the pace allowed us fully appreciate the grandeur of the *Barranca del Cobre*. The gorge is not much wider than the river and its facing cliffs rise six thousand feet straight up, giving the impression that they are about to meet in the sky. Occasional caves break up the cliff faces, some of them appearing to extend well back into the exposed volcanics.

We rounded one sharp curve of the snaking river after another until we came to a stretch that ran straight for nearly a quarter of a mile. Midway along this tranquil extent of the river was a patch of fine sand, a perfect shallow beach, for camp. The remainder of the afternoon was spent pitching the tent, gathering firewood, boiling water and enjoying a relaxed dinner.

As I was rinsing dishes in the river, Jose approached shyly, signaling a desire to broach a sensitive matter. I stopped what I was doing and invited him to bring up whatever was on his mind.

"I can make a fire but I cannot play a drum when the sun departs for the night," he said, almost whispering. "I have visited the man who makes the best drums many times and he is very kind but he will not sell me my drum for less than one hundred pesos."

"Where does he live?" I asked, making conversation while I tried to figure out what the boy was saying.

"Up at the top," he pointed, "not too far from the train station." He spoke a little more loudly this time. Although he stood straight and relaxed, he avoided direct eye contact.

I rinsed out the last dish slowly, trying to picture how the drum fit into the boy's life: *but I cannot play a drum when the sun departs for the night*. A matter of place within the community, perhaps. Or even a sign of leaving childhood behind.

"Is there some way I might help, Jose?" I asked gently.

He nodded, clearly relieved. "Could you pay me the one hundred pesos now for guiding you so that I could go buy my drum? I will sleep in my own bed and return in the morning."

I pictured him jogging all the way up to the top of the Copper Canyon in the dark so he could buy his drum. This wasn't simply like a youngster unable to wait to open a gift. This drum *meant* something within the culture. It was a symbol of something numinous.

I walked the dishes back to the tent and retrieved my wallet. Pulling out a hundred pesos, I knelt and handed them formally to Jose. Though he had never had so much money in his life, not a flicker of emotion crossed his face as he accepted the bills.

"Watch your step," I reminded him seriously.

He nodded, turned, and was off like a shot for the canyon rim.

I do not believe he took the long way.

TWELVE
1985

I had forgotten that it was *Semana Santa*. The *playa* was crammed to capacity with tourists from Guadalajara, come to celebrate Easter week in the quiet fishing village of San Blas. I wove my way inexpertly between the towels covering the beach while dodging all the partiers running, jumping and diving to catch, throw or chase various balls, Frisbees, and each other. It was sweet, although completely unexpected, pandemonium.

It had become my custom in the preceding few months to walk the mile-long playa in the early morning. I had become accustomed to walking the length of the beach, where it ended at a wide deep river entering the sea, in almost total isolation. It had been a rare morning when I'd seen another person strolling the lonely shoreline.

The utter transformation of the playa into a gathering of families and college students from inland was startling. The usual quiet of the morning was replaced by excited voices and blaring radios. The monotony of the beige sand was broken by the primary colors of swimsuits in motion. The flowing lines of the tide-washed playa were punctuated by innumerable mobile refreshment stands selling warm sodas and beers, fresh coconuts and milk, and smoked fish.

I worked my way down to the water's edge, where fewer people would make it easier to walk toward the river. I still had to watch out for everyone running between the sand and the waves. I still had a difficult time not getting distracted by all the bodies running, jumping, leaping, diving, and dancing everywhere. Sand and laughter and music filled the air. Amid so much noise and movement, I had to keep re-focusing my attention on my morning meditation of communing with the sea.

About two hundred meters down the playa I caught a kind of *nothing* out of the corner of my eye. An empty still point in the midst of all the commotion. I turned to see what had captured my attention.

Perhaps ten meters away from me, a couple kneeled in the sand facing the sea. Dressed all in white. In their mid-eighties. Hands clasped to their chests. Eyes closed. Heads bowed reverently.

A five meter circle of stillness enclosed them. None of the adults or children approached. No sand flew in their direction. No one dove to catch a ball near them. Yet all those activities were going on around them. Just not close enough to disturb them. Everyone carried on as if they weren't there.

I stood mesmerized. It was the most incongruous scene I'd ever seen. Then I remembered: San Blas was a sacred site for the indigenous Huichol, who made pilgrimages there at the spring equinox. The couple in front of me had kneeled there all night in a vigil leading up to their dawn ritual of throwing a sacred bundle into the ocean. They would kneel like this until sundown, waiting to see if the ocean accepted their sacrifice or threw it back onto the shore—if accepted, it would bring their people good fortune in the coming year and, if rejected, it would signal a year of coming hardship. The Huichol had been returning here for many centuries to conduct this ritual. It was a privileged sight.

Only a few moments had passed while I took this all in. Torn between admiration for their devotion and respect for their privacy, I was caught between staying and going.

Without any warning, the old man and old woman raised their heads together and opened their eyes in the same instant, looking directly into my eyes. There was a depth in their eyes that I recognized as the communion with the sea that I sought. My heart was swimming in deep water.

So subtle was the shift that I didn't take note at first. It all seemed so completely and utterly normal. The playa extended in both directions, wide and empty. There were no tourists anywhere to be seen. No refreshment stands. No plantation of coconut palms running up to the edge of the beach—just the wild jungle of the rain forest draped in tendrils of vines in its place. No cathedral spire rising on the horizon from the town square.

The breeze blew onshore at my back. The waves lapped at my ankles, washed away, came back. Gulls cawed in the distance. Frigate birds circled high overhead. A crab sidled between my feet seeking shelter from the gulls. It was all absolutely normal. If by *normal* we mean *six hundred years ago.*

I brought my attention back to the Huichol couple. Gaze fixed on their own horizon, their lips moved in a silent chant to the sea. Their faces betrayed no emotion. Their eyes simply poured out light.

On some invisible cue, they closed their eyes in the same moment and bowed their heads as one.

The playa snapped back into view. Families and college students ran riot across the beach, playing tag and catch. Radios blared. Laughter and shouts and sand filled the air. The palm plantation bordered the playa. The distant spire of the cathedral rose above the palms.

The elderly couple kneeled in the sand, praying for the sea to bestow its blessing. The commotion around them did not enter the invisible circle they occupied.

Even as the river at the end of the playa beckoned, the Goddess of the Ocean pulled me ever-further toward the open sea.

THIRTEEN
1955

It was the first time I saw *nothing*.

Up until that moment, growing up in the Ohio countryside had been mostly uneventful, filled with an unbroken string of days of play. The little farm was a half-mile from the nearest neighbors, its farmhouse one of those isolated structures breaking up the monotony of the Midwestern flatlands.

The only other thing breaking that monotony was the huge willow tree growing to the side of the house. It formed a perfect umbrella, its branches spreading out from its trunk and bending back down to nearly touch the ground. Having climbed up inside the tree, I was invisible from the outside. It was a world of calm and stillness, of swaying shadows, of long mornings watching cicadas emerging from their shell, of early evenings catching the fireflies lighting up the inside of the willow's canopy. It was my constant companion.

One night one of those fierce summer thunderstorms that grace the Midwest crashed and howled around us, rattling the windows with wind and thunderclaps. Flashes of lightning lit up my bedroom all night long, throwing strange shadows on the walls. Each time I drifted to sleep, another peal of thunder startled me awake.

The next morning, the storm had passed and left an uneasy calm in its wake. Opening the back door, I was confronted by the unimaginable. Where the willow had stood, there was nothing.

A bolt of lightning had struck the base of the tree and blown it apart. Limbs and branches were spread over the field but of the trunk there was nothing left.

I was looking through the space the willow had always occupied. I had not ever seen the farmhouses in the distance from the porch. Or the silos or barns. Or the highway leading to them. The willow, in all its fullness had always blocked the view.

And in one instant, that fullness had been transformed into an incomprehensible emptiness. How could something so big, so grand, so formidable, be wiped away as if it never existed? How could something so close, so intimate, so benevolent, be taken away so impersonally?

It wasn't that there wasn't something there—it was that the *nothing* that had been there all along suddenly revealed the world turned inside-out.

FOURTEEN
1990

She was the matriarch of the herd.

I poured out a couple pounds of rolled corn onto the ground and, though the younger deer all rushed forward to gobble down what they could, the herd parted to let her eat her fill. The general jostling for position went on without her. She was at least fifteen years old and all thirteen members of the herd were her descendants. We'd come to know her well, coming across her lying in the shade of the manzanita trees close to the house or standing on her hind legs pulling Spanish moss off the lower branches of the black oaks down by the orchard. She was already part of the land when we moved to our five acres in the country.

I rose at dawn the next morning and, looking out the kitchen window, saw her lying on her side next to the watering hole. Her breathing seemed labored and she did not appear to be resting comfortably. By the time I dressed and returned to the window, the rest of the herd was walking up on her. At first, they held back a few feet, straining their necks nervously for a sign of something familiar.

But such was not to be. The old doe's breathing relaxed and nearly ceased. The herd approached her cautiously, forming a circle around her. Several of the older does stamped their hooves plaintively. Each member of the herd bowed repeatedly, nuzzling her gently.

After a quarter-hour, her spirit had flown and the herd turned, reluctantly moving off toward the forest.

It was an honorable sendoff. I hope for nothing more.

FIFTEEN
1974

"You just want to relax and let everything go," Robert said like always.

I'd settled into the now-familiar position on the press bench. It was similar to being on one's hands and knees except all one's weight rested on one's collar bone on the padded bench. The only thing about the position that was slightly uncomfortable was the fact that one's head needed to be turned fully to one side—but that was an important element of the technique.

He stood over me, administering sharp, sudden thrusts to my spine with the palms of his hands. I knew he'd only stop once my back was undulating elastically, a mark that all my energy was flowing well and could withstand the press itself. "Good," he muttered to himself. "Good."

He repositioned himself. "Ready?"

I nodded, too comfortable to make the effort to speak.

"Okay, remember, pay attention. Take a deep breath. Here we go."

Robert placed his hands crossways to my spine, overlapping them so he could best focus the pressure. He brought the outer edge of his palm to bear between two vertebrae and began leaning forward in order to direct all his weight onto that single point. He held himself in suspension like that, waiting for me to exhale.

My breath escaped and he followed it, applying more and more pressure, pushing every bit of breath out of me, holding me in that state between breaths, pushing me past the point of caring about the next breath, and then suddenly withdrew his hands—

—and I catapulted out of my body like always.

A corridor lay before me, stretching into darkness, and I was soaring through it impossibly fast. Door after door flew open ahead of me. I moved faster and faster. The corridor turned slightly in a gentle arc. The dark dimly gave way to faint light. The corridor curved more distinctly, the light grew less dim, the last door burst open, and I floated above a plain of golden grasses. The sky shone gold, though there was no sun to be seen. The very air shone gold, as did the mountains framing the valley. Up ahead, a body of water shone gold as if the sun itself were rising from its depths. I flew toward it.

The golden lagoon lay before me like always. Exotic wading birds strutted through the shallows, periodically flapping wings to skim across the water. A teeming kaleidoscope of golden herons and egrets and storks and spoonbills danced an intricate choreography upon the stage of the lagoon. The golden air reverberated with their calls. I drifted just over their heads and from such proximity I could see clearly that each was a messenger. And that the call of each was its message.

I understood the meaning of each call and the meaning of all the calls together as they rose into the golden sky. Home at last, like always, I landed softly in the water and added my own call to the whole—

—and I was slumping off the press bench toward the floor, supported by Robert. He cushioned my fall, cradling my head until it rested on the carpet. I was fully awake immediately but he held me gently in place.

"Take your time. Try to remember it all clearly."

I replayed it several times before sitting up. "How long?"

He shrugged. "Two, maybe three, seconds."

"Seemed like hours," I said, shaking my head in wonder. I recounted the whole journey to him in detail.

"You still can't remember what you understood their messages to mean? Or your own?"

"Isn't that weird?" I replied. "It's all so perfectly clear when I'm over there."

"I'm not so sure that you can drag that kind of memory back with you. Or that that's even the purpose of journeying there. From what I can see, the purpose is to build up the strength and focus of intent to make the journey. The fact that you return to the same place every time reinforces the solidity of the vision. It isn't the same for everyone, you know. Most others jump around more, going somewhere new each time."

"I do not know why," I said, standing and walking over to where he sat at his desk, "but my soul really loves that place."

"Don't think it to death," he replied, shaking my hand. "See you next week."

SIXTEEN
1971

"You quiet your mind in order to reflect the quiescent state of the Oracle before a question has been asked," explained Master Khigh Alx Dhiegh. "This is called communion, or great sympathy, the way the diviner establishes rapport with the Oracle. This also mirrors the beginning of all things. Before the creation of this marvelous universe, the One Mind, the Tao, was an utterly still awareness. Only when thought arose did movement begin, initiating the birth of all things. The Oracle is ever like this and so is the mind of the diviner. Stillness is the resource. Movement is the response to need."

He opened his eyes, no doubt aware that my breathing was not falling in with his.

"Your mind is not still," he remarked drily.

"I remembered something yesterday. Something from my childhood that I had completely forgotten. It's a confusing image."

"Oh, good, I love confusion," he replied. "Let's hear it."

"It was the first week of first grade. We lived out in the country and I never went to kindergarten, so it was my first experience with public school. I was sitting in my seat before class began, drawing with one of those big thick lead pencils on a sheet of paper. Across the top of the page I had drawn a horizontal line, broken at one point near the right-hand corner to show that it was a trap door. Whether it was in the floor or ground, I couldn't say for certain. Descending from the trap door was a tunnel with a ladder leading downwards. A number of side tunnels led off to the left. Each of them was hidden behind a trap door of its own. All but one of those tunnels was booby-trapped with alligator pits or spears poking up into the air or quicksand. The one tunnel that lead safely through this maze ended simply in a room with a bed and a lamp. I completed the drawing with a real sense of satisfaction. Then a moment of recognition set in. I turned back through the notebook and saw the same drawing completed three other times. I realized I had already drawn this maze several times before and hadn't remembered doing so. That confused me and I never made the drawing again."

I shrugged self-consciously. "Now, here I am, fifteen years later, suddenly remembering an episode that I'd put entirely out of mind. And I don't feel any less confused about the drawing than I did when I was as a child."

He smiled reassuringly. "This is much more of a classic story than you imagine. You see, the *yang* spirit, the celestial spirit, departs when we begin to undergo social conditioning. Because this conditioning of the *yin* spirit results in the artificial self, the *yang* spirit withdraws into safety where it waits to be called back. Once it returns, it reunites with the *yin* spirit to produce the spiritual embryo of the true self. So, it was just natural for this to occur when you began to go to school. It is just very interesting that you were able to see this happening, that you could actually feel the *yang* spirit withdrawing into the safety of that room. I think the fact that you spontaneously remembered that event now means that it is time for you to call it back."

"Okay, that makes sense to me somehow. It sounds right. I'll try calling it back. Not that I have any idea how to do that. But it's a weird memory and it's left me unsettled. So I'll try anything, really."

"My own teacher said that the day you remember the name of your higher soul is a turning point," he said. "The moment it returns, it pronounces its name. This is a momentous reunion, where the lower soul recognizes the higher and their reintegration begins."

I must have looked as unsettled as I felt.

"Very well, go home," he waved resignedly, like a teacher releasing students for an early recess. "We work doubly hard tomorrow."

I bowed gratefully and made for my car. It was about a forty-minute drive home and all the way I kept thinking, *Come back! It's time to come back!* as if I were calling out across the inner landscape. The image of my childhood drawing kept appearing and I tried following the tunnel into the safe room, calling a forgotten part of myself back. Nothing happened.

I had given up on the exercise by the time I reached home. Precisely as I was making the U-turn to come around to my house on the other side of the street, however, I heard, as clearly as if someone were in the backseat, a voice say: *3+4 : 6+1 : return.* It was so loud and clear that I would have ordinarily jumped, startled.

But it was just as Master Khigh had said. I instantly recognized this name. Or formula. Or whatever it could be said to be. Odd as it was, it resonated so deeply that all my previous uneasiness evaporated on the spot.

I had seen a documentary on storks migrating many thousands of miles from Africa to Europe, where, after six months of being separated, the males and females reunited at the same nest they used yearly. The ritualized reunion, a dance marked by spectacular displays of affection, was a tribute not just to their bond but to the young they were about to bring into the world.

That was the image I had upon hearing my higher spirit's name. A ritualized reunion, a timeless bond reaffirmed, a dance of communion. Mates, long separated, reunited for the sake of the next generation of the lineage. After how long a migration had I arrived at the turning point?

SEVENTEEN
1987

The Australian Outback was flatter and hotter than I had imagined. Halfway between Darwin and Uluru, the highway ran through an interminable stretch of empty desert that had begun to look all the same. My wife, Leonor, and daughter, Melody, had given up trying to be interested in the monotonous scenery and opted for a nap in the back of the camper van we'd rented for a couple months.

The noonday sun through the windshield and the road's tedium combined to make it increasingly hard to stay alert. The narrow shoulders of the highway made it impossible to just pull off and I had to fight to stay awake until a wayside presented itself. It was just a gravel semicircle with several flat boulders that set it apart from the rest of the desert. I got out, walked around a bit to try to wake up, and then took up a lookout on one of the boulders.

In those days, I indulged in an occasional Turkish cigarette and took the opportunity to have a smoke. Sitting, somewhat like a lizard, on my rock afforded me a different view of the desert. What had appeared as empty and monotonous when driving sixty miles an hour took on an exotic feel—what I had mistaken for emptiness suddenly revealed itself as startling potential.

The stillness was broken by a movement off in the distance, its form obscured by the heat waves roiling off the flatiron desert. Whatever it was, it was coming my way and I couldn't take my eyes off it.

As it got a little closer, I could make out a giant red kangaroo slowly bounding through the heat waves. It was an impressive sight, blurred as it was, and my pulse quickened at the thought that it might pass close by. Squinting against the harsh sunlight, I tried to stare through the heat waves as it approached.

As it got a little closer yet, however, I could see that it wasn't a kangaroo at all but, rather, an elderly Aborigine jogging doggedly across the red sand. I could not have been less prepared for this transformation, as the figure of the kangaroo had seemed so substantial. Transfixed by the course of events, I felt myself being pulled into that altered state of the In-Between World. A brief *shift* of my center of gravity, marked by intense tunnel vision giving way to unobstructed peripheral vision, and I felt completely immersed in the timeless.

The figure that emerged fully from the heat waves had one more final transformation in store: the Aborigine I had taken for an elder was actually a young man trotting effortlessly in my direction. I had ceased being surprised, however, by appearances. With the *shift* behind me, the entire tableau had taken on the aura of normalcy.

"G'day, mate," he called out with a British accent. He wore nothing but a loincloth, although his torso was painted with white chevrons.

"Good day," I called back, waving.

He walked up and we shook hands before he took a seat on the rock beside mine. I offered him a cigarette, which he accepted formally, and we sat in silence, smoking and looking out over the vastness of the unbroken wilds. Not the hint of a breeze separated me from the desert air. The faint hum of insects seemed to be part of the silence. A row of small black ants marched in and out of a hole in the ochre sand. It wasn't that we were ignoring each other—it was more like we observed one another in our peripheral vision.

"You mind if I ask you a question, mate?" he asked conversationally. We might have been sitting on a bench waiting for a cross-town bus.

"Not at all," I replied, opening my hand in invitation. "Please."

"What are you going to be after you die?" he asked, all earnestness.

I took this as an invitation for less formality and turned to look at him directly. His face gave away nothing. He held himself at ease, one foot drawn up on the rock and an elbow resting on that knee. Meeting his gaze, I saw that his pupils were dilated—and that behind his eyes there shone a deep questioning. This, I realized, was the Aborigines' *Dreamtime* and the force that had pulled me into the In-Between World. That deep questioning in his eyes mirrored my own, I knew: neither of us were entirely sure that we were speaking to an actual human being.

"Well, now, until this very moment, I had never thought about it in that way," I replied equally earnestly. "Do you mind if I ask you what you've decided on?"

He nodded as if he'd expected this response. "Out there in the bush," he said, pointing back in the direction from which he'd come, "there's a ravine with a stream that comes out of a hill and runs down between red boulders and white ghost gum trees. In the morning, there's a breeze that flows up the ravine and in the evening, there's a breeze that flows down the ravine. After I die, I am going to be that breeze that flows down the ravine in the evening."

I nodded as if I'd expected this answer. "That way, you'll be with all your family and loved ones who are the stream that comes out of the hill and the red boulders and the white ghost gum trees and the breeze that flows down the ravine in the morning."

"So shall it be," he replied, making an odd fluttering motion toward the sky.

"So shall it be," I reiterated, adding my intent to his.

He stood and stared off in the direction he'd been heading.

"I'm on a walkabout, mate. You, too?"

"Yes, a vision quest," I replied. "On my way to visit Uluru."

"Uluru," he whispered. "May you find your gift."

"I have already found my gift," I replied formally. "Thank you."

"You have something for me," he said matter-of-factly.

I envisioned him crossing the Outback on his own, keeping the night at bay with the least of campfires.

"Tomorrow evening, the sky will hold a great spectacle," I replied. "The Sun, the Moon, Mars, Venus, and Mercury will all form a straight line in the heavens—and the remaining planets will form a grand triangle with them. People are gathering in sacred places all over the world to witness it. It is called the Harmonic Convergence and it is said that if one hundred and forty-four thousand people gather at the sacred sites and pray for universal peace, a new era of light will replace the old age of darkness."

He listened intently. "So shall it be," he replied, making the odd fluttering motion toward the sky.

"So shall it be," I reiterated, adding my intent to his.

"Fair trade," he concluded, shaking my hand. "A good sign for the walkabout. Now I must hurry if I am to reach a special place where I can witness this great event."

With that, he turned and set off trotting into the desert. It didn't take long before he was enveloped in the heat waves rippling off the red sand. I returned to the camper van before he turned back into a giant red kangaroo.

EIGHTEEN
1986

It was another wet landing. I clambered over the side of the launch, hiking boots and socks under one arm, camera bag under the other. The launch lurched at the last moment and I landed in breakers deeper than usual. Drenched almost to the waist, I struggled to keep my gear dry as I waded to the beach. Everyone else in the landing party had pretty much got their shoes on by the time I arrived.

"You must stay off to the side of the beach!" called out the Ecuadoran guide. "Sea lions can be very playful in the water but on land, this is their territory, they can be very dangerous!" He was a biologist and the strictest of the guides, making the excursions he led the least appealing to me. There were a couple guides born on the Galapagos who I greatly preferred—they loved to play with the wildlife and show off the natural wonders of the islands that were officially off-limits, which made their trips a true joy.

"Everybody, please! Get dressed as quickly as possible and withdraw to the far edge of the beach!" he yelled over the breakers and barks of the sea lions. He eyed me sharply. I was always holding up his itinerary.

"Oh, look!" called out someone in the party. "The poor thing's hurt!"

I looked up from my adventure in lacing my hiking boot while standing on one leg and keeping my camera out of the sand. A lone sea lion had advanced toward us, breaking away from the herd of about fifty engaged in sunbathing and quarreling over the best sunbathing spaces.

"What's wrong with it?" cried another person behind me, clearly distraught.

"Stay where you are! It may be aggressive!" shouted the guide, although he was really the only one remotely close to the creature. As the sea lion moved toward the guide in its odd lurching movements, I could see its profile. I understood all the concern. It *was* a disturbing sight.

Something foreign protruded from the sea lion's left nostril.

It was dark grey, nearly black, perhaps an inch and a half in diameter, about a foot long, and curved back on itself at the end. It looked for all the world like an over-sized fishing hook or one prong of an under-sized boat anchor. But it could be neither of those. Whatever it was, it was ugly and looked extremely painful.

The guide had turned around to warn everyone to stay where they were so when he turned back toward the sea lion, it was to find himself nearly face-to-face with it. He startled and the sea lion halted its advance, looking absolutely pathetic. You can hear about how the animals of the Galapagos have no fear of humans but it's impossible to imagine ahead of time.

"You have to help it!" and similar cries of, "Do something!" and "It's suffering!" arose from the group behind me. This was the guide who was constantly lecturing about how no one could interfere with the animals and how nature had to take its course no matter how cruel it seemed, so I didn't really mind seeing him put on the spot. Nonetheless, everyone yelling didn't seem to help the situation. Maybe to the sea lion it just sounded like the barks of his own herd but, whatever the reason, the guide seemed the more distressed of the two.

I could see the wheels turning in the guide's head as the sea lion inched closer to him. Nothing had really prepared him for this. Up until now, it'd all been theoretical. Animals were merely biological systems of responses to stimuli. The Galapagos was a laboratory for species and people must not interfere with individual organisms. And here he faced one of those organisms taking the initiative in a human-animal encounter and it seemed to have nothing to do with fight or flight.

The sea lion bobbed its head slowly, getting within arm's reach of the guide, who seemed suddenly oblivious to everything but the insistent creature before him. He cautiously reached out a hand and touched the awful-looking protuberance with a forefinger. Immediately, the sea lion arched and reared back violently. That quieted down the crowd on the periphery of the beach.

The sea lion came down on its front flippers and slowly maneuvered closer to the guide again, who was, understandably, taken aback. When it reared back, after all, it had been as tall as the guide. I gave him points for standing his ground.

It sidled up to the guide again and, again, in no way looked threatening. It bobbed its head as before and stretched out its neck, bringing the protuberance as close as possible to the guide. His curiosity seemed to have gotten the better of him and he reached out to feel the thing sticking out of the sea lion's nostril. No sooner than he had it in hand, though, than the sea lion reared back as violently as before.

And, as before, it returned to face the guide immediately, bobbing its head but otherwise utterly docile. The guide gave up on being cautious. Obviously, this creature wasn't just going to be ignored. And there seemed to be something else that had happened to the guide: he had attained a new status in the world by dint of being singled out by nature to interact in a special way. He could not help it. He had been transformed by the exceptional.

He grabbed hold of the protuberance, gripping it with all his will.

The sea lion reared back with its full force to its full height and the protuberance came free.

The guide stood there immobile, holding a dead sea snake by the tail.

It was over two feet long and the part that had lodged inside the sea lion was quite decomposed. The guide held the tail up at eye level until registering what he held, whereupon he dropped it in disgust.

For its part, the sea lion fairly skipped all the way back to the herd, barking with what sounded for all the world like joy.

I walked over to the guide and looked at his eyes. He appeared to be in shock.

"That was brilliant," I said.

"They must have collided and the snake became . . ." he mumbled distantly.

The rest of the landing party rushed up to him, hugging him and slapping him on the back, voicing their collective awe and approval. He scanned their faces one by one, finding a new reflection of himself in their eyes.

For my part, yes, I was privileged to have witnessed that display of animal intelligence—but even more than that, I was privileged to have witnessed the sudden and complete transformation of a human being.

NINETEEN
1987

The cuttlefish interrupted its quest for food in the tide pool to look up at me with obvious curiosity.

It was the first time I had ever seen one in the wild and had to hold my excitement in check so as not to make any sudden movements to startle it. We stared at one another through the clear water in a very odd kind of accord.

I stepped back from the tide pool and around the boulder lining it. Out of the cuttlefish's line of sight, I began waving energetically to Leonor, trying to get her attention down the beach. She had her head down, though, looking for seashells.

It was as lovely a beach as we had ever seen. On the eastern edge of Fitzroy Island, looking out onto the Great Barrier Reef of Australia, its tranquility above ground belied its teeming lushness under water. Whenever we weren't snorkeling among the reefs, we were scouring the beach for shells.

Leonor finally saw me waving and hurried the hundred or so yards to where I waited.

"You won't believe this," I told her excitedly. "A cuttlefish hunting in the tide pool."

We rounded the boulder slowly and approached the edge of the pool—but the cuttlefish was gone. Knowing how well they could blend into their surroundings, we looked hard, hoping to see it almost invisible against the sand or rocks. But no, the tide pool was empty.

Just as we were about to give up and turn away, the cuttlefish reappeared from around the far corner of the tide pool—accompanied by a second cuttlefish. They swam up to the middle of the pool and hovered, staring back at the two of us.

There is a language of things moving in space. A language spoken by all animals to varying degrees. Where bodies are subjects or objects, depending on their movements relative to other bodies. A language whose speaking is sometimes shockingly irrefutable: *While I went off to get my companion to share the experience, the cuttlefish did the same thing.*

TWENTY

1979

There are no level places in the Copper Canyon. To walk is to climb mountains, cross ridges, descend mountains, ford rivers, and then repeat as needed. The least chore requires strength and stamina. To walk for hours in such conditions is the norm—and is never considered a reason to avoid doing something.

"Ysidrio borrowed my horse this morning," Don Alfredo called out. "I think we better go see how they are getting along!" His smile hinted that he already had a pretty good idea how they were getting along.

We headed down river, into the canyon. It was a short walk of a couple hours. It would have been much shorter if I wasn't there, since Don Alfredo would have run the distance in a third the time. I could hike but I could not run like that. Don Alfredo didn't seem to mind at all. It gave him the chance to teach me about life and death in the Sierra Tarahumara. The day he had adopted me, he told Leonor, "I will teach your husband how to live here with just a small knife."

But to live there, as Don Alfredo perceived it, depended on the right attitude toward things. It meant treating everything correctly. Each time. Every time. It meant making the right decisions, especially difficult decisions, according to a complex code of the common good. And it meant taking personal responsibility for the consequences of every act.

He picked up a flat piece of volcanic stone and flung it like a Frisbee against the hillside about twenty feet away. With unerring accuracy, he'd cut a garter snake in half. It writhed in its death throes, oozing its insides. It still saddened me but I understood.

The first time I had seen him kill snakes like this I had asked him why. "These are beneficial snakes, Don Alfredo, they eat the pests that plague your crops." He replied diplomatically, knowing that I had a soft spot in my heart for snakes. After all, I had traveled all the way to the Copper Canyon with my pet ball python in tow. That had become a kind of reverse tourist attraction—all the Tarahumara up and down the canyon came to our tent to see the tame snake.

"Do you see any hospitals here in the canyon, Guillermo?" he had asked.

"No, Don Alfredo, I do not."

"Do you know of any doctors here that have medicine for rattlesnake bites, Guillermo?"

"No, Don Alfredo, I do not."

"Can you distinguish at a distance with absolute certainty between good and bad snakes, Guillermo?"

"No, Don Alfredo, I cannot."

"This is the dilemma, Guillermo. Let us say that I let a snake live because I know it to be a good snake but I make a mistake and it bites one of the people in the community. How am I ever to live with that guilt? Or, let us say that I let a snake live because I know it to be a good snake and later one of the people in the community is bitten by a rattlesnake. How can I ever be sure I hadn't made a mistake and it wasn't the snake I let live? How can I ever live with that kind of guilt?"

It had been one of his first lessons in the impeccable attitude.

We were removing our footgear in order to cross the river when Don Alfredo said, "Look there, Guillermo." I followed his gaze and saw a medium-sized orange-and-black butterfly among the rocks lining the river. One of its wings was broken.

"Why don't you pick it up and put it over there in those flowers?" he suggested. "You just have to be careful not to harm it any further."

I stooped to gently cup it in my hands but it managed to elude me, squirting through my fingers each time I thought I had it safely enclosed. After several times, I looked at Don Alfredo and told him, "I'm afraid if I try any harder, I'll harm it."

"That is how we are, too, Guillermo," he said. "Rayénari," and here he pointed to the sun god above, "Rayénari reaches down to pick us up and move us out of harm's way but we do not recognize it and so do everything in our power to continue as we were."

I stood and looked around. At my feet, the Rio Batopilas was starting its increasingly steep descent into the canyon lands below. To my left and right, the mountains framing the narrow river valley ascended nearly vertically to the exposed volcanic rimrock making up their ridges. This was an ancient highway for the Tarahumara, in use for thousands of years. Their ghosts passed through me, trotting up and down the canyon. Mountain lions and coyotes stalked prey among the boulders and manzanita. I loosened my senses as Don Alfredo had been directing, visualizing a great pair of antennas growing from my head, reaching all around to touch, to taste, everything hidden in my surroundings. From the cloudless sky, Rayénari reached down, cupped us in his hands, protecting us from harm on our journey.

"Ysidrio's ranch is just around this bend in the river," said Don Alfredo, stepping into the clear cool water.

We forded the snaking river and followed it around where it opened up on a small sloping hillside that had been cleared of rocks and cultivated. Higher up, a rough house of stacked rocks in the fashion of the Tarahumara grew out of the rock wall of the mountain. Don Alfredo motioned for me to be quiet and follow him stealthily.

We worked our way closer to the field, crouched down behind a rise. Don Alfredo carefully raised his head and looked toward the field. He stifled a laugh, motioning me to take a look. As carefully as possible, I took a look. Ysidrio was trying to plow, pleading with the horse to obey the reins. But the horse was pulling him around as it wished, carving s-shaped furrows in the soil. It was horribly comic.

"That horse is a real trickster," said Don Alfredo, picking up a couple good-sized rocks. "Now, jump up when I do and scream like a demon."

On cue, we leaped from behind the rise and shouted wildly.

"Hyah, horse!" yelled Don Alfredo angrily, throwing his rocks with uncanny precision at the horse.

The result was no less comic: the horse immediately began pulling the plow perfectly straight and Ysidrio waved a casual *thank you* over his shoulder as if he'd been waiting for Don Alfredo's intervention.

I was pulled down behind the rise right away. "We have to hide so the horse thinks the same thing could happen any time," Don Alfredo explained. We crept away as we came, crouching out of view until we rounded the river bend.

"Funny horse," I remarked once we were out of sight.

He nodded. "Every animal has a soul. Some are very wise and some are foolish. Then there are those like that horse that are some of both. He is smart enough to know how people will react and he is foolish enough to think that making life difficult for people is fun. He demands respect but has to be reminded sometimes to return that respect. Ysidrio respects him but doesn't have the relationship to demand respect back. Animals are just like people. People forget this and treat them differently. We are all souls in the eyes of Rayénari."

To be a shaman, in Don Alfredo's mind, meant a soul being fully integrated into nature.

TWENTY-ONE
1979

It was the most beautiful saddle in the Sierra.

Decorated with polished silver on the horn cap, the skirt corners, the cantle, the conchos, and stirrups, it glinted in the sunlight from across the canyon. Its leather was tooled in intricate carvings of wild horses on the plains bordered by stamps of acorns and oak leaves. The cantle bindings and saddle strings were masterpieces of rawhide braiding. It had been custom-made for Don Julio down in Parral and was his pride and joy.

He rode erect and dignified astride his favorite quarter horse that day, the very picture of a distinguished *caballero*.

"Quira-va!" called Don Luis, whose home doubled as the only post office in a hundred miles. "Why don't you come in and have a soft drink, Don Julio—it's going to be a long hot ride back to your ranch!"

"Quira-va!" replied Don Julio, giving the horse a nudge with his boots. "But it will get too late in the day if I stop and talk!"

Don Luis shrugged. "I understand! You have no time for old friends now that your ranch is a success!"

Don Julio hid his irritation. He could see that Luis was hurt but found it unseemly that he gave voice to it like some country bumpkin. There was nothing he could do but stop and visit—it would not do to leave these feelings hanging in the air.

"You are right, old friend!" he called back to Don Luis. "Work isn't everything! I need to relax more! Let's have a soft drink and visit like old times!"

Grudgingly dismounting and shaking hands, he followed Don Luis into the house whose front room had been converted into the post office and a small store selling the warm soft drinks and stale snacks that arrived once a month with the mail.

No sooner than they had stepped inside the cool of the adobe house than they heard a tremendous explosion just outside the door. Rushing back outside, they found Don Julio's famous saddle fused in a smoking mound of silver, leather, and the remains of his horse.

Out of a clear blue sky on a sunny day, a single lightning bolt had struck his beautiful saddle and blasted his favorite quarter horse into unrecognizable bits.

Neither Don Luis nor Don Julio had to say anything. One more minute in that saddle and Don Julio would have shared his horse's fate. If not for Don Luis' insistence, Don Julio would have met the same gruesome end. If not for humbling himself, no matter how grudgingly, to accommodate his old friend, his remains would have been fused with the saddle and horse that he had flaunted so shamelessly.

After that, the two of them were inseparable. They shared a bond others could imagine but not fully grasp, having not had the experience of such a tangible brush with death.

Never was there a more contrite or sincere friend than Don Julio. He wouldn't be appeased until he had convinced Don Luis to move to his ranch in the highlands and take over the responsibilities of foreman there. Don Julio always swore in the years that followed that the success of the ranch was due to the fact that he never made a decision that went against the judgment of Don Luis.

•

This is the story Don Alfredo recounted as an example of a butterfly allowing itself to be picked up and carried to safety.

TWENTY-TWO
1970

I was waiting. That was all.

A friend was coming over to pick me up and I was waiting out in the front yard. It was one of those impossibly perfect days. A light breeze, warm sunshine, blue sky.

It was a simple joy to just be waiting.

I was gazing East at the cloudless sky when I gradually became aware of the *presence* of two vast beings beyond the sky. Their identities were self-evident: it was the masculine creative being and the feminine creative being. And their relationship was equally self-evident: all of creation was the child of their union—and their union was the result of their love.

I lowered my gaze, to more fully take in their creation.

Looking at the yard beneath my feet, the thought leapt to mind spontaneously: *I am a blade of grass in an infinite field of grasses.* The comfort of belonging that accompanied this thought was, like warm sunlight, part of the impossibly perfect day.

I was waiting. That was All.

TWENTY-THREE
1970

"Please excuse the mess, but we're just starting to get moved in."

It was absolutely the most unfamiliar way of talking I had ever heard. The voice lilted, doubled back on itself, contradicted itself, parodied itself, all seemingly effortlessly. It was a kind of formality of the East that was simultaneously subverted by irony from the informality of the West. It was the most sophisticated communication I had ever heard. What it really said, so clearly it astounded me, was, *Don't excuse the mess, isn't it all wonderful, I'm really pleased to finally be moving in here!*

He crossed the room, extending his hand gracefully. "Khigh Dhiegh, rector of the Sanctuary."

His was an imposing presence. Though not especially tall, he was quite stocky. With a nearly perfectly round face, shaved head and vaguely Chinese features, his visual appearance alone was unusually striking. It was his mannerisms, however, that were magnetic. His voice and gestures seemed perfectly self-contained, his diction flawless, and his words impeccably chosen.

All that I might have been able to ignore if not for the way he turned the full brunt of his attention on me while he spoke. His tone of voice struck a precise balance between superior experience and respectful deference. He was already 60 years when I met him at 19, yet I was made to feel as though my presence mattered in the larger world. This was the first person I had ever met who lifted my gaze above the horizon and I had known him only a few minutes.

Sitting across his desk from me, he described the newly founded Taoist Sanctuary and I Ching Institute. There were going to be classes in martial arts, tai chi, qi gong, and so forth, taught by Master Share Lew, and there were to be various classes in the *I Ching* that he would be teaching himself. He described the prices of the courses and their tentative schedules and the opening date of the Sanctuary. He was polite and jovial, making me comfortable as he extended a very warm invitation to return once classes started.

He stood, shook hands again, and saw me out into the warm Southern California morning.

My head was spinning as I returned to my car. I sat in the driver's seat for long moments, trying to get my thoughts and feelings in yoke. I picked up the pages I'd left on the passenger seat and stepped out of the car. I felt slightly disconnected from my actions, as if my body had decided on a course of action and I was merely along for the ride.

I knocked on the office door. Upon opening it and seeing me standing there, a look of bemused curiosity crossed Khigh Dhiegh's face. He didn't say anything. He just let his expression speak for him, allowing me time to speak. I was quite surprised by what I had to say.

"You are the first person I've ever met who thinks about the things I do. I know it is an imposition on your time but I wonder if you would be so kind to look at these few pages I've written?"

His expression changed. He became quite serious and for a moment I thought he was going to decline. I cannot imagine what he saw at that moment but he looked deep into me and decided to accommodate me. Waving me inside, he returned to his desk and reached out for the material I'd brought along. He quickly scanned the first page, then the second a bit more slowly, and the third more slowly yet. Then he started over, reading the first page slowly and intently.

I had been studying the *I Ching* on my own for a year at that time and had been as intrigued by the structure of the symbolic system as I was by the philosophy it expounded. As a result, I had hit upon a series of correlations to the *I Ching* involving chess, binary mathematics, some of the social sciences, and several art forms. The pages I had handed him formed the outline of a game I would eventually create called Intrachange, or Esoteric Chess.

He paused occasionally in his reading to ask me a question. Why did I use this word? Where did I get this idea? How did I make that connection? I answered as best I could but it mostly came down to following my intuition. He finished reading it, scanned it again briefly, then set it down in front of him.

When he finally looked at me again his eyes were watering.

"I wasn't sure you were going to find me," he said emotionally.

I must have looked perplexed.

"Do you know who I am talking to?" he asked warmly.

The room took on a different atmosphere, as if time had suddenly stopped. I had the distinct impression we were inside one of those glass balls you could shake to make a snow scene. Everything was suddenly made of crystal, timeless and pregnant with meaning. Events were occurring in my vicinity that my rational mind could not keep pace with at all.

"Almost," I replied slowly. The word seemed to come up out of the ground through the soles of my feet. I was in an utterly unfamiliar state that *almost* felt familiar.

"Good," he replied slowly. "Good. You can begin coming to see me right away. We have much work ahead of us."

"Yes, sir."

He came around the desk and took my hand in both of his. "This is a very auspicious day for both of us," he said with such genuineness that my heart cracked open in sudden recognition.

There, bent over me with such affection was the face of my teacher, Master Khigh Alx Dhiegh.

TWENTY-FOUR
1973

"We came here to San Blas to die," Harry Green explained jovially.

His wife, Carol, nodded enthusiastically beside him. "We met in the oncologist's office and just fell in love right away," she confided. "Two months later, we were married."

"Yes," agreed Harry with the mock gruffness of the middle-aged man interrupted by his wife. "So we sold everything, quit our jobs, and moved down here. Why should we spend the last months of our lives in the Colorado winter?"

"I was a nurse. Harry had a very popular talk show on the radio in Boulder," Carol said proudly.

Harry waved it off. "Not that big a deal," he said, obviously pleased that she'd mentioned it.

They were an other-worldly looking pair. He was tall and thin, with thinning white hair and a thin, scraggly white beard. She was short and round, with thinning brown hair. His face was long and narrow, hers was round and cheery. He was in his mid-sixties and she in her mid-fifties. They did not give the impression of being entirely in their bodies.

They had rented a house in town but came regularly to the restaurant in the little hotel on the beach that we were running. As their health declined, their appearance became more gaunt but they never showed a downturn of spirit. Their visits became less frequent but always enjoyable—we would coerce them into staying after the restaurant closed, making sure to fill them with good conversation, laughter, and beer.

One night, as they were climbing into their Mercury convertible and saying their goodbyes, Harry took me by the elbow and said seriously, "We're having a small ceremony tomorrow night. We'd really like it if the two of you would come."

•

The next evening was balmy with a light breeze. Harry and Carol sat out on their porch waiting for our arrival. All the lights in the house were off but the living room glowed dimly in candlelight. They were both dressed in long blue robes that displayed no markings. Their manner was uncharacteristically subdued although they greeted us with graciousness and warmth. We followed them indoors, adopting their demeanor of seriousness.

Four large throw pillows were arranged in a circle on the floor of the living room. Candles occupied strategic positions around the room, including one at the top of the circle near an open bottle of wine and a Bible. Empty cups sat in front of each of the throw pillows. Harry took the seat by the Bible, motioning for Leonor to sit to his left and me to his right. Carol entered the circle and poured each of us a half glass of wine from the bottle before taking up the pillow across from Harry.

"I guess I am what you might call a mystic Christian," he said, smiling in the dancing candlelight. "Many years ago, I was taught the importance of caring for the dead souls who are lost in the afterlife. As part of that practice, I was taught this ceremony, called the Rainbow Bridge Invocation, which is a means to help the lost souls find their way and cross over to paradise. I've been teaching it to Carol and we would like to pass it on to you before we go."

I glanced at Leonor, who nodded her assent, and replied just as formally, "It would be our honor."

Harry beamed and raised his cup high. We all followed suit.

"We dedicate this ritual to the service of all souls," intoned Harry in his most professional radio voice. "May all those seeking the way home find it here now!"

He drained his cup solemnly and we all followed suit.

"Now, all souls who can hear me, all souls wandering in the quagmire of a life past, all souls lost and confused on a road that keeps circling back on itself, all souls who can remember but cannot make sense of where they are or why they are repeating the same acts over and over again, all souls who are drunk on anger or hate or lust or grief, all souls who have had their lives stolen from them, all souls who have stolen the lives of another, all souls cowering in fear, all souls parading in conquest, all souls following others, all souls convincing others to follow them, and all souls who have forgotten that they are children of the one creator who is continually calling them home! Now, all souls who can hear me, listen to the mystic song!"

Harry's sing-song delivery was trance-inducing. Even the candles seemed affected, sputtering brighter and throwing larger shadows on the walls. Leonor sat cross-legged, meditating with her eyes closed.

Picking up the Bible, he turned to a bookmarked page and began reading the twenty-third psalm in a solemn cadence:

"The Lord is my shepherd, I shall not want.
He maketh me to lie down in green pastures.
He leadeth me beside the still waters.
He restoreth my soul.
He leadeth me in the paths of righteousness for his name's sake.
Yea, though I walk through the valley of the shadow of death,
I will fear no evil, for thou art with me.
Thy rod and thy staff they comfort me.
Thou preparest a table before me in the presence of
   mine enemies.
Thou annointest my head with oil.
My cup runneth over.
Surely goodness and mercy shall follow me all the days
   of my life.
And I will dwell in the house of the Lord forever."

I'd never been much of one for the Bible but I had to admit to myself that if I was a lost soul in the afterlife, these words might just be among the best I could ever hope to hear. They seemed, in actuality, to be tailor-made for the occasion.

Harry set the Bible back on the floor and snuffed out the candle before him. Lifting his head suddenly, he whispered in surprise, "There! Do you see it? It's taking form! The Rainbow Bridge!"

This seemed to be Carol's cue and she cried out, "Oh, it's so magnificent! The bridge of many colors! The red and yellow and green and blue! Its light is growing stronger!"

"Its light is growing stronger," repeated Harry.

The candles died down a little as a breeze passed through the room.

Harry looked off to the right, behind me, and whispered sharply, "There! Do you see them? They are beginning to arrive!"

"Look at the joy on their faces! They see the Rainbow Bridge!" cried Carol emotionally.

"They see the Rainbow Bridge," repeated Harry.

The candles flickered lower, the shadows danced higher. I couldn't say exactly when, but somewhere during the ceremony, I had made the *shift* to the In-Between World.

In the dark a light had taken form, shimmering like a mirage at first and then fleshing out in transparent reds and golds and blues. Faint as a will o' the wisp, it leapt high, arcing far into the deep, directly over Leonor's head. I felt footfalls approaching from behind me.

"Now, all souls come to the Rainbow Bridge!" intoned Harry. "Welcome! Welcome! Your loved ones await you on the other side! Here is the path home you have been searching for!"

"Look!" hissed Carol excitedly. "Soldiers from the revolution! Children looking for their parents! Spanish conquistadors! Indians dead from foreign illnesses!"

"Now, all souls from all times and all places," chanted Harry, "there is nothing stopping you from hearing me! There is nothing stopping you from stepping onto the Rainbow Bridge! There is nothing stopping you from rejoining your loved ones! There is nothing stopping you from leaving the darkness and pain behind!"

"Roman legionnaires and Mongols and Huns and people from every part of the world who have died in wars, who have died of plagues," whispered Carol sadly. "All the victims of violence and accidents and life-taking illnesses." She continued on like that for several minutes, enumerating the multitudes appearing before her eyes.

Throngs of transparent flames did, indeed, approach the Bridge and were carried away, transported, to its other end nearly immediately. A glowing bonfire burned brighter and brighter at that distant end. I could not say how Carol was identifying them but I could attest to the high emotions that seemed to be flowing from them.

"They are passing over," said Harry with relief. "They are passing over to the other side."

"They are passing over," repeated Carol exhaustedly.

Harry closed the Bible and relit the candle. The vision faded, a dream escaping into forgetfulness upon waking. Carol shifted stiffly on her pillow. Harry poured the last of the wine into his cup and downed it in a gulp.

Leonor opened her eyes and stretched. "That was so beautiful," she said. "I could almost see it just the way you were describing it."

Harry unwound his legs slowly and tried to stand. I got there quickly and helped him to his feet.

"Damned cancer," he muttered, glancing at me sideways. "I'm getting weaker. Can't hold the bridge open as long as I used to."

"It was perfect, Harry," I replied, supporting him by the elbow as we made our way to the porch. "Thanks for passing it on."

He smiled wryly. "Wasn't altogether altruistic, you know. I need someone I can trust to perform it for me, just in case I get stuck there."

"Consider it done," I whispered in his ear as Carol and Leonor joined us, another bottle of wine in tow.

Harry sighed contentedly. "It's been a good ride."

We all lifted our cups to that.

TWENTY-FIVE
1973

We had descended to the heights of Creation.

The sun angled lower, illuminating the canyon walls in the richer colors of the spectrum. Water riffling through well-worn pebbles soothed eyes and ears both. The river was low at that time of year and we were able to make our way out to its middle by jumping from one exposed stone to another. Standing there with the river flowing gently around us, we watched the last rays of the sun let go of the cliff face until morning. Standing there at the bottom of the *Barranca del Cobre*, far from even a remote outpost of civilization, we were immersed in the sacredness of nature.

Dusk set in and, just as we were about to return to the sandy river bank, the sky turned unexpectedly dark. A huge black cloud suddenly covered the entire sky of the quarter-mile stretch of the river. But it did not stay in the sky where clouds belong—it sank lower and lower at a startling speed and, as it got within a thousand feet or so, it appeared to boil and bubble from within, constantly changing shape. Within just a minute or two, it had reached the canyon floor.

Bats. Millions, literally millions of bats. A single shadow of millions of fluttering shadows that extended all the way around the serpentine bends of the river. A single shadow of so many bats that it darkened the sky. The air was so thick with bats that there seemed no room between them.

Yet they never touched us. Certainly, they came close. Within inches. Hundreds swarming within a half-dozen feet of us, wings rising and falling in slow motion so close we felt the wind on our skin. On several occasions, one hovered directly in front of my face, looking into my eyes, as curious as wary. For our part, we were as wary as curious. We did not move a muscle, standing stock still on the flat river rocks, not daring to confuse the swarming creatures for fear of causing them to collide with us. But they essentially ignored us.

They had come to drink. Hanging suspended as if on invisible strings, they fluttered just over the surface, lapping up water with their tongues like small winged puppies. They came in waves: one wave of tens of thousands of bats hovered in place, lapping water for ten or fifteen seconds and then flapping off, replaced by the next wave. Wave after wave lowered into place, drank, and made room for the next wave.

It was all over in ten minutes. The great shadow evaporated into the sky as quickly as it had appeared. As if it had never been there. We took a breath—the first, it seemed, since the bats' arrival. Only then did it register how frozen in place we had been. We made our way back to shore, sitting in the soft sand, savoring the Great Mystery forever around us.

From high above, the echoes of drums danced among the towering cliffs.

•

We awoke the next morning to the heartbeat of a drum.

And the smell of breakfast.

It was just getting light but the aroma of frying fish convinced us we were wide awake.

Jose sat on a rock, watching the fish cook while he pounded lightly on his new drum. It was big enough for him to hide behind.

"I arrived early and caught some catfish for breakfast," he announced, taking a break from his drumming to turn the fish. "I hope it was okay to wake you."

"It smells wonderful, Jose!" Leonor exclaimed. "You are a marvel!"

"Here, son, let me see what your hard work has brought you," I said, gazing pointedly at the drum.

The pride with which he presented his prize nearly brought tears to my eyes. Clearly, it represented a turning point in his young life.

He and I examined every inch of the drum, its stitching and skin and decoration, while Leonor took over the preparation of breakfast.

It was an extraordinary meal. Swallows flitted around the campsite, catching insects. The morning chill was giving way to the lowland's humidity. The sun made its intentions known. Jose was beyond himself with joy and we were delighted to have contributed to his life in such a meaningful way.

"Oh, you'll never guess what happened last night after you left," Leonor exclaimed, telling him about the bats and how exciting it was.

His reaction was not what we expected.

"The bats fly ahead of the rain," he said ominously.

"The trail," I replied.

He nodded. "A little rain will make the trail very difficult for the climb back to the top. A big rain will cause the river to rise unexpectedly and make staying very dangerous."

•

We broke camp and began our ascent within half an hour.

The climb was the hardest thing we were ever to do our entire lives.

The switchbacks were steep and interminable. The humidity was stifling. The sense of urgency was overpowering.

After an hour or so, Jose offered to carry Leonor's twenty-pound backpack for her. She gratefully relinquished it and he carried it the remainder of the hike. He also carried his oversized drum, of course, which he played continuously until we reached the plateau above. It was more than a little discouraging to watch as he disappeared around a mountainside and to hear the drumbeat fade into the distance as he outpaced us effortlessly. Eventually, the sound of the drum would grow louder again as we approached the place he sat waiting for us to catch up.

We kept moving because we had to. The thought of trying to finish the climb on a muddy and slippery trail—a trail that was defying our best efforts under favorable conditions—kept us moving long past the point of exhaustion. After ten hours, we were falling asleep between steps and still had hours to go before reaching the top. We pressed on because we had no choice. The sky was darkening and the smell of coming rain filled the air. Step after plodding step, we marched dreaming.

After thirteen hours, we reached the rim of the canyon. A light rain accompanied us on the hour-long stroll on level ground back to the train station.

While we waited for the train, the rain set in hard, attended by long forks of lightning and sharp cracks of thunder.

We sat on a wooden bench beneath the shingled overhang of the station. Jose sat on the other side of Leonor, tapping his drum lightly in rhythm to the rain. Next to me, Jose's father carved the neck of a violin out of pine. He nodded slightly when I said, "He's a good boy."

TWENTY-SIX

1995

I was burning up. I'd picked up a vicious cold on the bus from Monte Alban to Xochicalco. I couldn't hold a thought for more than a few seconds. I hurt all over. My head was full of mucous. I alternated every fifteen minutes between shakes and chills. I was freezing.

The motel near Xochicalco normally would have been fine. But the way I felt, it was depressing and confining. Nonetheless, I should have just holed up there, stayed covered and sweat it out. But the walls grew closer by the minute. Far away from the world of reason, I could only see irrational answers. I stood out on the highway and waited for a taxi to flag down.

The driver agreed to come back and get me when the ruins closed. The sun was blazing hot even in the early morning. I resolved to burn the cold out of my body by day's end. Every stone block or bench became my sunning place. I lay on my back on the heated stone, arms outstretched to welcome the full force of the sunlight. I felt like stubborn metal between anvil and hammer.

Slowly, the sun began to have an effect. My head cleared little by little and strength gradually returned to my legs. I began actually looking at the ruins, wandering around the vast grounds, awed by the heads of the feathered serpents protruding from the ancient temple foundations. Everywhere I looked, men dressed in white linen bent nearly double, trimming the grass with practiced swings of their machetes. The ruins employed a large contingent of groundskeepers to keep the grass low for walking.

On previous visits, I had not made my way down to the smallest of the three ball courts and always resolved to do so one day. That day seemed to have come. The long walk did me good. Xochicalco, the healing place called *House of Flowers,* known for its ancient sweat baths, was working its magic. By the time I reached the ball court, I was feeling like my old self.

It was by far the smallest ball court I had ever seen. It seemed impossibly narrow and short to have allowed the kind of physical combativeness associated with the Mesoamerican ball game. The stone seats surrounding the ball court came down so close to the playing field that those watching would have felt more like participants than spectators. I could not, especially, see any possible distance between the spectators and the sacrificial victim at the end of the game.

I took a seat on the lowest tier of benches, soaking in the warmth of the sun. I tried to imagine the players jostling for position with the hard rubber ball. I tried to picture the intimate stands of the arena filled with cheering supporters in all their jeweled and feathered finery. I tried to glimpse the cosmological significance of the ball's movement through the stone goal.

I bowed my head, letting the sun hit the back of my neck, baking the last of the cold out. I noticed that the groundskeepers had been here the past day or two. The thick summer grass was cut very short and impressively even. Upon close inspection, I saw that the grass was trimmed right down to the ground cover, which had small clover-like leaves and lovely lapis-colored flowers. Once I had paid close attention, in fact, I was surprised that I was just noticing the flowers. They were everywhere, fairly blanketing the ball court.

The lightest of breezes kissed the field, causing the little blue flowers to shudder slightly, their petals lifted on the wind. The whole of the field came alive like that, simply and naturally as could be imagined, for the lapis flowers were not flowers at all—they were tiny cobalt butterflies that came awake as one when stirred by the breeze.

The whole of the ball court suddenly filled with thousands upon thousands of the butterflies as they all rose into the air at the same time. They hovered for a few moments like a thick blue cloud at eye level before slowly rising and dissolving into the cloudless sky.

I seemed to have stepped into mythic time. I stood and walked out into the middle of the ball court. It felt like walking through ghosts.

I knew that when great warriors of ancient Mexico died, they went to the house of the sun for their well-deserved reward—and that after four years, they returned to this world in the form of butterflies and hummingbirds to inspire and encourage the living. I had the distinct impression that I had just witnessed the return of thousands of those ancient warriors, who came back into this world through the very flowers whose nectar they would drink. It only made more sense that such a transformation would occur on the cosmological battlefield of the ball game.

All the way back to the waiting taxi, I inspected the grass, looking in vain for a sign of the lapis-colored flowers. Every groundskeeper I came across told me they had not seen any such flowers in the whole of the ruins. For a change, I had more answers than questions.

TWENTY-SEVEN
1974

"Have you ever heard of the *nagual*?"

Without waiting for me to answer, Robert began setting pen to paper. He drew a circle in the middle of the scrap paper and looked up at me, one eyebrow cocked expectantly.

"I've heard of it, yes," I replied slowly. I wasn't as interested in talking about what I already knew as what he wanted to teach me.

He looked at me skeptically but waved off that conversation for another time.

"Here's what we've learned from *the press*. This circle represents our personal awareness," he said, drawing over it several times, giving me time to get oriented. He then very methodically drew two much larger ovals attached on either side of the circle.

"Here, on the left, is what is called the *tonal*," he explained, tapping that oval. "It's what we might call ordinary consensual reality. The world everybody knows. On the right, however, is the *nagual*, the non-ordinary reality of shamans and mystics. The thing is, this is also a consensual reality. It's an autonomous world of shared intentions."

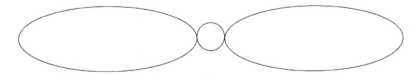

He tapped the circle again and continued, "So we find our personal awareness here in between what we might call the natural and super-natural worlds. At any given moment, we are free to move into one or the other but, of course, modern cultures place much more emphasis on occupying the *tonal*. The truth known to the old ones, though, is that the *nagual* is no further away than its twin, the *tonal*. It just takes a very different kind of intention to enter it."

He looked up, found me staring at the drawing. "With me so far?"

I nodded pensively. For all its simplicity, the drawing accorded perfectly with my experience. I could, in fact, even sense the two realms off to either side of my awareness.

"Now what begins to happen as we gain more experience with the practice of shifting between the *tonal* and the *nagual* is that our personal awareness becomes less and less a personal identity and more and more a child of the marriage of the two realms." He'd turned the scrap paper over and redrawn the two ovals, this time so that they overlaid in the middle of the page.

"This is what is happening to you now that you've been learning to shift back and forth. Your personal awareness is becoming identified with the aspects of the *tonal* and *nagual* you are experiencing."

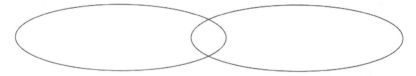

"And this is what happens after many years of practice," he said, re-drawing the ovals a final time.

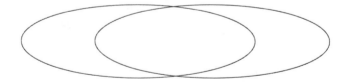

"As shamans and mystics become more intimate with the two worlds, they actually become identified with the marriage of the *tonal* and *nagual*. Their own nature becomes the nature of the two worlds and they cannot be told apart. In this way, they assist in the embodiment of the two realms becoming perfectly identified with one another."

He turned the scrap paper back over again, tapping on the original drawing.

"The important thing is to see that the *tonal* can also be thought of as the world of manifestation and the *nagual* can be thought of as the world of archetypes that gives birth to manifestation. In this sense, the *tonal* seems to be much more fixed and solid, where the *nagual* seems to be much more fluid and dreamlike."

"Why are you saying they both 'seem to be' more this or that?" I asked.

"Because the *tonal* only seems to be more difficult to change—and the *nagual* only seems to be easier. In order to change the *tonal*, we have to work in the *nagual* with its archetypes rather than working directly in the *tonal*. On the other hand, there are many many other intentions at work in the *nagual*, so just because it is more ethereal doesn't mean it is more amenable to changing direction or momentum. It is also a consensual reality and its other co-creators need to be reckoned with."

I shook my head in bewilderment. "I've just got a toe dipped into the ocean," I said, appreciating the enormity of the work.

"Well, let's see if we can't dip a few more toes in today," Robert replied, nodding to the press bench.

TWENTY-EIGHT
1970

"I'm having a little dinner tomorrow night. I would appreciate it if you would attend," said Master Khigh Alx Dhiegh after a particularly long study of the *I Ching* hexagrams. This was not his way of actually *asking* me to do something.

I arrived the next evening to find the large table in the meeting room set for a gathering of some dozen persons. All the plates and serving dishes and utensils were from China. The smells of aromatic vegetarian dishes filled the room. Large candles illumined the scene. Master Khigh appeared, carrying a pot of fresh tea, wearing one of his robes magnificently embroidered with dragons and tigers.

"Ah, good, good, come and join us," he said, motioning to a seat in the middle of the table.

I took my seat, caught between appreciating the beauty of the setting and wondering what it was all about.

He stood at the head of the table, smiling warmly, allowing his eyes to come to rest on each of the chairs. "Before we enjoy this wonderful repast, let us make our invocation," he said formally.

Opening his hands and stretching them out to his sides palm up, he intoned, "In the oneness of the past, present, and future, we have already awakened to our true nature! It is so! Now, my fellow Buddhas and Bodhisattvas, it is my honor to bring together such an auspicious gathering of great-souled ones! May all benefit from our communion!"

He clapped his hands three times ritualistically, then turned to me and asked me to help him serve the food. He handed me the smaller of the two serving bowls and had me follow him around the table, adding rice to each of the plates after he had served the vegetable dish. We worked our way around, serving his plate last and then taking our seats.

Closing his eyes and making a bow to the food before him, he said, "May the nourishment we are blessed with here increase the blessings of all beings." I repeated his gestures and words.

His demeanor immediately changed from serious to merry-making. Picking up his chopsticks, he announced jovially, "Enjoy! Enjoy!"

I was in the middle of chewing my food when Master Khigh asked, "What is the meaning of the order of the hexagrams?" I struggled to swallow in order to answer, although I had nothing to say but admit my ignorance—but to my surprise, he was not addressing me. He had turned to his right and asked the chair next to him. He nodded, listening attentively, as he politely continued eating. He seemed to be about to say something else but looked down and across the table to another chair, listening to what seemed further explication of the first answer.

The evening progressed in that manner, with Master Khigh asking technical and philosophical questions of his guests, two of whom he called by name—Chu Hsi and Shao Yung. He seemed particularly interested in how to establish better rapport with the Oracle and asked each of his guests to address that matter specifically. With each successive question and *listening*, I could better sense the presence of *others* with us in the room. Clearly, Master Khigh had entered the In-Between World and was enjoying the company and conversation of the sages.

As we were finishing the meal, he turned to me and asked if I had a question of our guests.

There *had* been something I'd been wondering about for some time and so asked, "Why aren't there readings for the *unchanging* lines?"

Master Khigh hissed and called out in surprise to the table at large, "Hai! Now you see why he is my student?"

He turned to the chair to his right again, absorbing the answer and nodding thoughtfully. It suddenly occurred to him that I might not have heard the answer and he said, "The reasons are essentially historical and amount to an oversight. He says you will rectify that oversight in this lifetime."

This was the manner in which Master Khigh Alx Dhiegh taught me. It was the manner in which he introduced me to his own teachers. It was the manner in which he showed me how to address questions to the invisible sages accompanying us always. And it was the manner in which he assigned me tasks that would make up my life work.

TWENTY-NINE
1950

Christmas Eve. I was nine months old. My father, just twenty-one years old, was carrying me up the icy steps to his parents' home in Columbus, Ohio. He slipped and we fell. It was a bad fall. Both my legs were broken and I was placed in the hospital with both legs set in casts and raised in traction. I remained in that situation for more than two months. At that age, I would ordinarily have been learning to crawl and developing physical mobility. Circumstances, however, dictated I learn a different kind of mobility.

THIRTY
1969

It sounded like a gunshot. I stepped out of the dorm into a group of young men circling a young African-American teenager lying on the asphalt. He was dying quickly, having been cut in half by a shotgun at close range. A shotgun wielded by the elderly security guard hired by Pepperdine to keep the boys away from the girls' dorm. Of late, he'd been given the added assignment of running off the neighborhood kids using the basketball court before the university team needed it for practice. Everyone had always laughed about Charlie and his shotgun. Everyone knew it wasn't loaded.

I turned around, packed my things, threw them into my car, and drove away.

I figured I'd learned what I came to college to learn.

THIRTY-ONE
1958

The walls were pale green. The linoleum was scuffed and scarred. The air was full of antiseptic and voices over loudspeakers. The bench was wood and uncomfortable.

Beside me sat my grandmother, whose principal function in life at the moment was to instruct me in the art of not fidgeting.

"Don't fidget," she said again.

My maternal grandmother raised seahorses. She also raised me for a while and loved me greatly.

But this wasn't that grandmother. My paternal grandmother did not approve of her son's marriage to my mother and so passed that disaffection along to me in sternly disquieting ways.

"Don't fidget," she said again.

Neither she nor my grandfather had told me why we were going to the hospital. They'd just woken me in the middle of the night and driven in silence.

My grandfather liked me, so I was sorry to see him disappear behind a pale green door, leaving me to sit in the hallway with my grandmother.

My grandfather's family were hillbillies from West Virginia. He managed to put himself through dental school by carrying hundred-pound sacks of potatoes from the fields to the train depot. He was a big man, six-and-a-half feet tall, with broad shoulders and big, soft, dentist hands. He seldom spoke. He laughed through his nose. Whatever he did, you knew he meant it.

"Don't fidget," my grandmother said mechanically.

I was eight years old. My principal function in life was to fidget. I had to let something out or explode.

"Where's grandpa?" I asked timidly.

"He's in there with your great-grandfather," she replied tersely.

I took this in slowly. It seemed significant. I hadn't known my great-grandfather was in the hospital. Ever since I'd known him, he lived upstairs in my grandparents' house. He was confined to a wheelchair and had lapsed into dementia before I was born. A veteran of World War I, he sustained injuries that resulted in gangrene and the amputation of both his legs. He was already a ghost when I knew him, so we got along famously. I would rest my back against a wheel of his chair and read aloud to him. Occasionally his hand would drop and pat my head.

The pale green door opened and my grandfather stepped into the hallway.

He was sobbing. His chest heaved. Tears and snot ran like a waterfall. His back was bowed. His head was bowed. He moaned, lowing from inside some dark cave.

It was the first time I ever saw what strength is.

THIRTY-TWO
1969

It was another unbearably hot day in Tucson. But I did not miss Southern California. My folks had moved there when I was ten and I left as soon as I could manage. Left for good. The tragedy at college was just the capstone on a pyramid of bad memories. After a childhood in rural Ohio, the culture of Southern California had held a nightmarish quality. I'd moved to Tucson to spend time with a cousin and find my way in the world. I'd gotten a job as a counselor at a boys' ranch on the outskirts of town and seemed to have found my calling. I would follow this line of work, determined never to return to the Los Angeles area.

It was another unbearably hot day and I had an hour before I needed to be at work. My one-room apartment was set in an old motel that had been converted to a small apartment complex when the freeway had bypassed it. It had a bathroom. The kitchen was a hot plate and a miniature refrigerator. But it cost sixty dollars a month and it was within walking distance of work—two selling points for someone without a car who was taking home three hundred dollars a month.

I laid down on the bed with the ceiling fan set to high. I stared at the whirling blades, content to be where I was. I had no urgency. No anxiety. No uneasiness with my surroundings. I was in a routine of my own making. I had been counseling at the boys' ranch for months and found others appreciating my work. Everything had been stripped down to its simplest form, I was self-sufficient and it was all different enough that I realized it.

I stared at the whirling blades of the ceiling fan, letting the breeze wash down over me.

I closed my eyes.

I was standing on a narrow ledge on an impossibly high steep cliff face. A magnificent river valley of lush vegetation sprawled below. The piercing cry of an eagle alerted me and I turned to see a huge golden eagle hop from the ledge, spread its wings and soar off hunting. I leapt off the ledge, spread my wings and soared off, scanning the ground below for prey—

—my eyes snapped open and my body jerked, startled to be lying face-up where I had just been flying face-down. Adrenaline slammed into my nervous system and I lurched upright, panting.

I walked to work and gave notice, leaving in a week to return to Southern California. Within a few months, I met my future wife, Leonor Alicia Ramirez-Oropeza, and my teacher, Master Khigh Alx Dhiegh.

THIRTY-THREE

1979

I had never been so drunk.

There are three distinct phases to the Corn Harvest Ritual and this was the third: the *tesguineria*, where the community gathers to drink all the *tesguino* they want over the course of three days.

There is a drinking game the Tarahumara like to play with newcomers, who they designate the guest of honor. To honor the guest of honor, each of the twenty or thirty partiers gets around to offering the guest of honor a drink of tesguino from the ceremonial gourd. Which holds about a quart of the freshly fermented corn beer. Which the guest of honor must drain before refilling it and offering it back to the person. There were many more of them than there were of me.

Tesguino, or *batári* in Tarahumara, is still fermenting when you drink it. Just in case you are ever the guest of honor at a tesguineria. It is still fermenting when you drink it and you do not think you are going to get drunk, no matter how much you drink. It is quite refreshing, even if a little gritty. More people come to honor the guest of honor, who cannot ever get drunk on such mild beer.

I followed Don Alfredo out to the field, where he showed me how to induce vomiting in order to empty the stomach and make room for more tesguino. After some period of time, we repeated this procedure. As did everyone else there, of course. The day went on forever. There was music. Laughter. Clapping one another on the back. The normal reserve of the Tarahumara gave way to an openness and outgoingness I had never seen before. They were like different people. The tesguino allowed them to drop their reserve for a few days every year.

The day never ended. Time stood still. There was a point in the day where everyone seemed to arrive at the same emotional state. It was like a wave of ecstasy that carried us all along with it. I do not think it could be attributed wholly to the tesguino, which seemed to give the Tarahumara the excuse to transcend the everyday seriousness of survival and return to their innate sense of joyousness. It was a certain type of spirit that had to be released. After thousands of years of ekeing out a living in the desolation of the Copper Canyon and five hundred years of repression by the Spanish, the Tarahumara had adopted a demeanor of impenetrable seriousness of purpose. That was the face outsiders saw, it was the face they showed each other on a daily basis. Only during the traditional celebrations, with the permission granted by the tesguino, could they let their souls shine through.

I had played music with a band and fallen into a beat with the other musicians that picked us up and carried us along with it. That had always been the purest moment of communing with a group of people I'd ever had. Until the tesguineria at Don Alfredo's ranchito. That day, celebrating the harvest of corn that would carry the community through the winter, I found myself part of an ecstatic unity that was the very embodiment of spiritual rejoicing.

But it came at a price. I had never been much of a drinker. And days of tesguino took their toll on me. I got alcohol poisoning, was sick for a week or two. And have never been able to have more than a single drink since then. It was a small price to pay, however, for gaining entry, even for a brief time, to the ancient ritual space of sacred intoxication.

THIRTY-FOUR
1993

The echoes of precisely detonated dynamite caps ricocheted off the cliffs embracing Tepotzlán. The daily competition to see who could bounce the most echoes back and forth against the facing precipices had begun. It was deafening, blanketing the town every sunset in waves of thunder that made conversation impossible.

I sat at my favorite restaurant, *Coquis*, savoring the sonic chaos along with an after-dinner cappuccino. It was a small place, just the front room of an old three-story home across from the plaza. It had only four or five tables and catered primarily to locals, the favorites of which were invited through the back curtain leading to the courtyard beyond.

It was perfect for my needs and, since I'd been a regular for a couple months, I was ignored and allowed to read and write in privacy. Sitting there at the table by the door, I had an intimate view of the street scene around the town plaza and its ever-changing traffic of tourists and street vendors. Every day I would drag my ragged copies of the codices into *Coquis* and spend hours poring over them in the most pleasant circumstances imaginable.

The owner was a small wiry man surrounded by a cadre of real eccentrics. He attracted them and they spent even more time at his place than I did, mostly back in the hidden courtyard behind the curtain. Every afternoon two or three of them would appear and compare times with him. Nineteen minutes, one would say. Eighteen minutes, another would say. Sixteen minutes the owner would say. It took me weeks to figure out what they were talking about: these were the times it took them to climb the cliff up to the ancient temple dedicated to Quetzalcoatl. The one time I had made the grueling trek, it took me an hour and a half. I, of course, went up the series of switchbacks that made the hike possible for ordinary human beings. These extraordinary competitors were racing straight up the cliff on their secret ascents. Their climbing the cliff face was always dedicated to the prehispanic patron spirit of Tepotzlán, *Two Rabbit,* the ancient god of intoxication.

The sun set gold and purple on the cliffs, twilight passed into night and the explosions died down and echoed away. I had lost track of time, absorbed in the Codex Selden, and hadn't noticed the street emptying early. An approaching storm thundered off behind the cliffs and a wind was rising, whipping the plastic sheets of the vendors' booths into a frenzy.

"Why do you come here every day?" the owner asked from behind my chair. It was the first time he'd ever addressed me outside the usual routine of ordering and paying for food and drink.

I turned and looked up at him. His expression was absolutely neutral. He reminded me of someone who is not really going to listen to your words but to your tone of voice.

I smiled only slightly and spoke as if to Don Alfredo. "I like the atmosphere of your home, it makes me feel very comfortable, it is very agreeable, I am able to get work accomplished here and still be in the middle of the community. I thank you for your hospitality and hope I have not overstayed my welcome."

He received this formality and nodded acceptance.

"You are a student of the old ways?" he asked, pointing at the codices with his chin.

"I am fascinated by them," I replied.

He studied my face hard. He came to a decision.

"I have something to show you," he said solemnly, waving me to follow through the curtain. I scooped up all my material and carried it with me into the courtyard. The lights in the town flickered off and on again in the storm. We turned to the right abruptly and he motioned me to set down my papers on a table and placed a folding chair on them against the wind.

A slatted door on antique hinges gave way to a steep narrow stairs. It wound around tightly in a series of right angles, passing the doors for the second and third floors of the house. At the end of the stairs, a ladder led to the roof. This last part of the climb was in near complete darkness—only the faint light entering through the open trap door to the roof provided any illumination. It was a relief to exit the claustrophobic stairwell.

A number of young men and women were all standing around waiting as we scrambled off the ladder and onto the tar paper roof. They all wore lightweight windbreakers of various colors, in preparation for the storm, I reasoned. The owner donned a similar jacket and handed me one. The wind was starting to really howl and the rain couldn't be far behind. I accepted the breaker gratefully.

Without any sign I recognized, we were all suddenly standing in a circle. At that range, I could recognize many of these young people as those who regularly passed through the restaurant and on into the courtyard.

"Do you know what *Coqui* means?" he asked me, having to yell to be heard in the storm.

"I believe it is the old Zapotec word for *royalty* and even *divinity*," I yelled back, trying to make myself heard to everyone there. They all responded by touching two fingers of their right hands to their left arm, just below the shoulder.

"For centuries, we have kept the old ways alive—we are the children of Ehécatl!" the owner cried out against the wind. It took a minute for this to sink in.

The children of the wind god?

They broke out of the circle and moved to the edge of the building facing into the wind. They spaced themselves evenly, extending their arms out to both sides. As if on cue, the wind rose to a pitch and each one of them stepped to the very edge of the roof, spread their arms wide, and leaned out over the edge into the wind. In an act of sheer faith, they were allowing themselves to be completely supported by the force of the rushing wind.

But that was not a sufficient demonstration of faith. One by one, they grabbed the corners of their opened jackets, pulled them out wide and, catching the wind, were lifted on the air back to the center of the roof. Some skimmed the rooftop, just a few inches above it. Others floated several feet above the tarpaper. Two, including the owner, rose well over six feet into the air before closing the "wings" of their jackets enough to drop softly back to the roof. They were all whooping at the top of their lungs with wild joy but they could barely be heard.

The first drops of rain began to spatter on the tarpaper and they all raced back to the edge of the roof to repeat their flight before the rain and lightning arrived. This time, I could make out what they were shouting while carried aloft: *Ehécatl! Ehécatl! Ehécatl!*

"One of these days, you fly with us!" each of them said, shaking my hand once we had returned to the courtyard. I accepted their words appreciatively, replying, "It is a joy to see such courage still alive today." We were all smiles, the air smelled of ozone and pent-up electricity, the world seemed about to vent its birth-cry.

After that evening, I never ate out in the public restaurant area again. I took my food and studied my codices behind the curtain, in the courtyard where I was to meet the *patolli warriors* and, through them, the gods of the four directions.

THIRTY-FIVE
1971

There is nothing quite so lonely as the sound of a fading train whistle echoing off snow-draped mountains beneath a full moon.

Such was our love-at-first-sight with the Sierra Madre Occidental. Standing there at the train station in Creel at two in the morning, we watched the train pulling away across the valley and wondered at the poignancy of the moment. The entire world glistened in crystalline moonlight. The mountainsides were covered in snowy pines. The air was still, sounds carried forever. The train, our last contact with the modern world, called goodbye.

We wondered, too, at our lack of planning. All we knew about Creel was that it was an old timber town at the top of the Sierra. We didn't know if there was anywhere to stay. Or to eat. It was just renowned for being the jumping-off point to the Copper Canyon. The station was closed and utterly deserted. And it was cold—we were at nearly eight-thousand feet elevation and there was two feet of fresh snow on the ground—and the whole town was dark. We could see the whole town: the one street, a dirt affair turned to frozen mud, ran alongside the train tracks for a couple hundred yards.

Just as we were considering unrolling our sleeping bags and huddling in them until morning, a figure came down the hill and introduced himself as the night watchman for the station. Although he had obviously just pulled himself out of bed, he was pleasant enough and offered to show us to the only hotel in town.

The *Hotel Nuevo* was closed, too, of course, but eventually the owner pulled himself out of bed and opened the door. A huge fireplace was still burning four-foot logs and the warmth was soul-heartening. The prices for a room were more than we could afford and we despaired of having to return to the winter night after warming in the benevolence of the fireplace. But the owner relented, saying he had a small cabin at the back of the hotel that was for staff when needed. He offered to rent it to us for a few days at a much more reasonable rate.

We could not have been more pleased. It was utterly homelike. A small log cabin with a huge bed and good-sized fireplace. There was firewood stacked in the room and thick hand-woven Tarahumara blankets stacked three-deep on the bed. We felt sorry for anyone having to stay in one of the hotel rooms.

The next morning was brilliant, if chilly. We found the little dining area and had some breakfast, chatting with the owner and his staff. It turned out we were his only tenants, as there were seldom tourists in Creel and almost none in the winter. As we knew next to nothing about the Tarahumara, we listened eagerly to his experiences. The hotel was really more like a trading post and he had all kinds of wares made by the Tarahumara for sale. What interested us the most, though, were his stories about the depths of the Copper Canyon, where there still existed the *Cimarrónes*, the Untamed Ones, living as their ancestors had for millennia, with only minimal contact with the modern world.

•

The first *Cimarrón* I ever met was the great Tarahumara runner, *El Ocelot,* The Jaguar.

His Spanish name was Bárnabe and he was superhuman. While not especially tall, he was one of the most imposing figures I have ever laid eyes on. His waist and hips were narrow but his torso broadened out to a barrel chest and extremely wide shoulders. His calves and thighs were simply immense. At a distance, he had the gestalt of an inverted triangle set on two tree trunks. He could run hundreds of miles without stopping and was a ferocious competitor in the Ball Game played among the Tarahumara.

I met him that afternoon in Creel, where he was walking through deep snow wearing sandals and a loincloth. He had come up from the bottom of the canyon, from his home in Batopilas, to sell a violin he had made. Close up, I could see that his front teeth were missing, the result of being struck by the hard pine ball during one of his early races. It was hard to imagine him as a fierce competitor—his mannerisms were so deferential and his voice so soft, one might take him for an accountant or librarian. If not for a physiology that appeared to be a throwback to the Aztec warriors of old.

The violin was handmade, glued together with pine pitch. The bow was carved from a single branch with horse hair ingeniously attached. I offered to buy it but I'd left my wallet in the cabin, so he agreed to accompany me back there to get some money. I invited him in out of the winter weather and he accepted cautiously. Once he saw Leonor by the wood stove, however, he relaxed and seemed comfortable.

While waiting for me dig out the money, he noticed a handmade wooden flute I traveled with. He asked to inspect it, so I handed it to him, explaining that it came from Bolivia. He was fascinated by it and immediately began measuring it in order to reproduce it. All the measurements were in units of his fingers, hand, and arm: the flute itself was this portion of his forearm; the holes started the length of his hand from the mouthpiece; the holes were one knuckle apart; and so on. He committed each of the dozen or so measurements to memory without any apparent effort.

Knowing he was from the bottom of the canyon, where it was like springtime even in winter, we told him there were lots of blankets in the cabin and he would be welcome to make a place for himself by the fire.

He smiled appreciatively but declined, saying shyly, "I have never slept indoors."

Making his farewell, he shook my hand in the traditional Tarahumara way—by pressing my fingertips gently between his thumb and fingertips. Watching him disappear into the winter dusk, I was left with the sense of having just crossed paths with the most solid, most present, person I had ever met.

❊

The Sierra itself made such an impression on our souls in that first visit that we could not stay away. The spirit of its people so captivated us that we kept returning until I met my teacher, Don Alfredo, and became part of his family.

•

As for Bárnabe's violin: it hung on my wall for decades until I made a gift of it to a friend. To the best of my knowledge, it still plays as well as ever.

THIRTY-SIX
2010

"The first thing you have to do is catch a hummingbird with your hands," the Navajo runner was telling us.

Resting near the bottom of Canyon de Chelly, we were greeted by the young man, who had already passed us twice before as he raced up and down the steep switchbacks of the canyon's 600-foot cliff.

"It never changes," he explained as he pulled up in front of us, barely breathing hard. "My great-great-great-great-grandfather was a famous runner and now all the men of our family keep his tradition alive."

He launched into his story as if we'd known one another many years, his smile warm and pleasant, his gaze steady and sincere.

"He passed on *the form* that our family follows in order to get the strength to run up the canyon walls. After you catch the hummingbird, you must hold it between both hands until it calms down. This teaches you patience because it might take a couple hours before it trusts you. Then you open your hand and let it perch there so it knows you are going to let it go. While it sits on your hand, you sprinkle corn-silk-pollen on its wings and wait for it to fly. As soon as it takes off, you have to run through the cloud of corn-silk-pollen that it leaves behind. I was able to complete *the form* when I was sixteen years old and that is how I earned the strength to run up and down the canyon," he concluded, automatically pointing out the ancient route up the cliff that shortcuts the modern switchbacks.

The young man's presence struck me as forcefully as did his physical prowess. Family, clan, memory, and land: he had a sense of identity and place supremely rewarding to witness. He brought to mind something a priest once told me about the Tarahumara: *Their biggest sins are smaller than our smallest ones.*

The next day we traveled to First Mesa in the Hopi Reservation. It is a remarkable place, a narrow plateau high above the high desert. Visitors cannot enter without a local escort and absolutely no photography of any kind is permitted. A series of three small villages perch atop the mesa, the last one, Walpi, being the oldest. Occupied continuously for the past 1,100 years, it maintains its traditions by not allowing any electricity, phone, or other modern conveniences.

"From here, you can see the sacred mountains where the Kachina spirits live the other half of the year when they are not here," the young Hopi woman told us, pointing off toward Flagstaff. "The village is much more lively while the Kachinas are here. It seems so lonely when they leave in July." Her eyes teared up at the thought of the Kachinas' departure the following month.

I followed her gaze to the distant mountains, trying to imagine how the village anticipates the Kachinas' return every February. Family, clan, memory, land: she had a sense of identity and place that is supremely rewarding to witness. She brought to mind something Don Alfredo often said: *The land itself is spirit.*

Out in the inter-mountain deserts, the storm clouds sail across the landscape, trailing veils of rain that shimmer in the harsh light of the sun. At night, coyotes bay at the sliver of the moon and owls hoot at the edge of clearings. The land stretches on forever, mirrored by the blue sky in the day and the clear stars at night. *It never changes.*

The road runs through spirit without end.

A couple days later, we stopped at Bryce to walk down into the canyon. At Sunset Overlook, a woman's hat flew off over the railing and landed on the sheer slope of the cliff. Immediately, her male companion crawled over the fence to retrieve the hat. Gallant or not, it was foolhardy in the extreme: his tennis shoes slipping on the loose gravel, he clung to the mesh fencing with one hand while reaching for the cheap tourist hat with the other—all the while oblivious to the 500-foot drop below. A backpacker in worn hiking boots turned away, grimacing apprehensively: "Is that piece of crap really as valuable as his life?"

Like a souvenir photo, the whole journey snapped into sudden focus.

There are two different worlds. One is populated by people who know the value of life and hold it sacred. The other is populated by people willing to leap out on the edge of self-destruction in exchange for meaningless trinkets.

The high desert wildflowers were in glory that season. After a long wet spring, the sun was calling out all the hidden blossoms from the red sand. They were soon to be gone. It was such a privilege to be present while they celebrated life. How short it all is.

The final night, we camped in Valley of the Gods. It is an ancient sacred site not far from Monument Valley. Half a moon washed the towering monoliths of sandstone in cool white light, casting deep shadows on the night. The wind meandered through our tents warm, cold, warm, cold. The evening star set reluctantly behind a sandstone behemoth. No cities, not even towns, for many miles: the stars shone bright as possible, the zodiac stared back at us like the edge of the galaxy. Gnarled junipers danced in the moonlight to the timeless chanting of crickets. It was impossible to sleep when the whole desert was dreaming.

•

It was so quiet you could hear the mountains' prayers spilling out of their world into the other.

THIRTY-SEVEN
1975

"You had them, goddammit! You had them and you let them go!"

The lightest possible drizzle coated the asphalt in an oil-on-water sheen that reflected the streetlights in running colors. The high desert air smelled fresh and clean, relishing the rain. The drunk shouting at me flicked his cigarette out into the night and lit another one while he glared at me.

This was why I didn't frequent bars or taverns. But I'd received an invitation to meet some locals interested in setting up an alternative school for at-risk youth, so I'd decided to attend. The meeting had devolved into a beer fest and, needing to take a break outside for some air, I'd bumped into the inebriated philosopher in the parking lot.

"You had them on the ropes, they had nowhere to hide. And you just didn't have the guts to finish them off." He was a history professor and had mistaken me for the official representative of the counter-culture. The Sixties had caught the power elite completely by surprise, he lectured. They were slow-moving and unable to adapt to the shifting values of modern civilization. There had not been an opportunity to conduct a nonviolent revolution on that scale in hundreds, no thousands, of years. Hearts and minds were being won over at a rate unimaginable a decade before. The young had hit them in their blind spot, revealed their moral corruption, shown their claim to authority to be illegitimate—and then let up, thinking the war was won on the battlefield of abstract ethics.

"They won't make the same mistake with you," he snarled contemptuously. "They will run you to ground and make you regret your high-mindedness." He turned on a heel and went back inside. Music from the juke box escaped before the door closed behind him.

The drizzle let up. A sliver of moon came out from behind the clouds.

Headlights scarred the desert hillsides when cars turned off the highway. I told my feet to head for the car but I stood frozen in place, unable to shake the drift of the professor's words.

Sometimes it's the short and random exchanges in life that make an impression. This chance meeting taught me much about divination, for it went directly to the matter of predictable backlashes—and it did it in the most practical way imaginable. Real life politics, whether on the grand scale of culture wars or the small scale of personal relationships or the individual scale of inner transformation, was nearly universally prone to repeating cycles of action-backlash-action-backlash.

Sometimes even the best-intended actions provoke the worst-intended backlashes. But predictable—that was the issue. If an action wasn't conducted in the correct manner or if it wasn't carried through to the end or if it overshot its mark, then the backlash was predictably inevitable. As the years passed, I found myself increasingly grateful for the professor's lesson because he had called my attention to this process of change with an example I had lived through—and, of course, because his words only proved more accurate with time.

Sometimes you have to go down to the local bar or tavern just to be reminded that truth seldom tastes sweet and that prophets are seldom sober.

THIRTY-EIGHT
1990

I was going the wrong way again.

"There's lightning strikes out there on the point!" exclaimed a woman in khaki hiking shorts and good solid hiking boots.

"It's dangerous back there," a man in khaki hiking shorts and good solid hiking boots assured me.

"Don't go out there—it's hailing!" declared an elder in khaki shorts and good solid hiking boots.

Everyone in the crowd rushing past me seemed to agree: I was running the wrong direction.

But the chance to be in the middle of that kind of a storm on the North Rim of the Grand Canyon proved irresistible. I picked up my pace, hoping to get out on the vista point while the storm held together. I'd seen similar phenomena in the Copper Canyon, where the hot air at the bottom of the canyon rose, hit the cold air up at the rim of the canyon, and developed into small, very local but very powerful, hailstorms.

The trail through the mesquite and pine forest ended abruptly at the rimrock vista. I dropped my rucksack at the edge of the clearing and walked out to the precipice. An iron railing, about waist-high, was set into the sandstone—definitely the most attractive lightning rod in the vicinity.

I found myself gulping air and realized I was breathing heady ozone. My hair was floating in a surreal halo, made suddenly weightless by the static electricity suffusing the place. Both signs of one of the possible poles of a lightning strike.

But I was transfixed.

The vista was situated on a side canyon, a few hundred yards from its junction with the main canyon off to the right. It was a relatively narrow canyon, less than half a mile across, facing the mile-high sheer sandstone cliff opposite it. Beyond that, a perfectly flat plateau, unbroken by any mountains, that extended all the way to the horizon.

A serpent's tongue of lightning flicked, striking a pine on the opposite wall of the canyon. The smell of ozone grew stronger again and I was not reassured by the ring of pines all along the rim of the side canyon—a huge percentage of them showed signs of past strikes, their bark stripped in a spiral where the lightning had run down their trunks. The thunder, of course, was so close that you felt it more than heard it.

I had arrived just in time. The dark, roiling, storm cloud was more than halfway across the side canyon, moving away from me. It was one of those miracles of the high desert—not a great weather system that blankets an entire region, but a highly-compact, small-scale storm, perhaps only hundreds of yards across, that can be just as violent in their own way. It rumbled again but I did not see the corresponding lightning if there was one. It receded all too quickly toward the opposite side of the canyon, where it would begin to break up once it got onto the plateau.

I took the opportunity to approach the iron railing and lean over to see the bottom of the canyon just below. A shallow stream meandered from left-to-right, on its way to merge with the Colorado River. I leaned further out over the railing and could see that the source of the arroyo wasn't too far off to my left, where it descended a steep fissure in the otherwise monolithic cliff face.

Already, the storm cloud was losing its organization. It had stopped hailing altogether and the intensity of its surroundings was diminishing: the air held neither the ozone nor static electricity it had. As the cloud approached the opposing cliff, the shadow it had cast on the canyon floor passed and the sunlight hit the wet sandstone and set the stream afire.

At first, I thought it was opals glinting in the shining water. But I quickly realized it was one end of a rainbow, shimmering on the surface of the stream as if struggling to make itself visible. Then, it abruptly came into focus, whole and complete: an enormous circular rainbow.

I gripped the railing against a moment of vertigo as the rainbow burst into existence all at once, a great ring of color two miles across. Its lower half leapt off the stream a mile below, where its two ends nearly touched, mere meters apart. Its upper half arced across the clearing sky, framing the near emptiness of the vast plateau running away to the horizon.

The vista point looked directly into the center of the glory. I seemed for a moment suspended at the midpoint of the perfect circle of the world's spectrum. Time did not so much stop as become encased in amber: the absolute transience of the moment splintered eternity, creating its own being, independent of all other moments, outside the bubble of creation.

What did stop was the mind, of course. Several minutes passed without producing a thought. The light did not produce a thought. The sky did not produce a thought. The Grand Canyon, a surprising symbol, did not produce a thought. I did not produce a thought.

What did not stop, however, was the heart. Several minutes passed where the heartbeat of everything within that drop of amber fell into the same perfect rhythm, entrained to the same perfect count of *one-one-one-one . . .*

The minutes did, inevitably, pass and with them the light and with it the rainbow. It faded reluctantly, like one of those ennobled lovers in a movie, keeping the promise to *not look back*. I turned, picked up my rucksack, and struck the trail back to the road, no less numbed than if I'd been struck by lightning.

Halfway back up the trail, I started encountering a long line of hikers going the opposite way. "Is it safe again? Did the storm pass? Is it safe back there?" they asked as they passed me.

THIRTY-NINE
1970

"Look at these young people teaching after their first enlightenment," Master Khigh Alx Dhiegh complained, naming a couple of the more prominent recent returnees from India.

"I don't know, they sound pretty good to me, Master Khigh."

"That's because you can't hear the nuances," he replied curtly. "Teachings have to address specifics, not mild generalities."

"But the truth—" I protested.

"Truth!" he exclaimed indignantly. "Mark my words, it won't be long before you've got all kinds of enlightened people just repeating the same old sutras and scriptures over and over! When will they make it their own?"

I scratched my head in exaggerated perplexity. "But shouldn't the truth be universal?"

"What medicine is universal?" he asked pointedly. "Truth is medicine, it has to address specific illnesses. An elder and an infant may both have pneumonia but you don't give them the same medicine or the same dosage. You don't give the same medicine to people who have different illnesses. Different cures are prescribed depending on circumstances of season, age, gender, past conditions and general vitality. And then there is the problem of medicine turning to poison if taken too long. Not to mention the problem of prescribing medicine for someone who is perfectly well. Truth is exactly like this."

"Truth as medicine . . ." I repeated, trying it on for size.

"Don't you know the story of the monk who asked the master, *Please give me a word of truth,* and so the master replied, *Your mother is ugly.*" He suppressed a smile, trying to drive his point home. "Just being able to say the truth is not the same thing as saying *the* truth that helps the other. It needs to help them untie knots. It has to help them resolve their unease."

"So these people bringing back teachings aren't really helping others by sharing what they've learned?"

"Maybe they help some. But they definitely mislead others. Their own understanding hasn't stabilized yet and here they are teaching right away." Master Khigh looked out the window at a distant memory. "When my teacher initiated me, it was only after I took a vow to wait thirty years before teaching. *The tea needs time to steep,* he would always say."

I was speechless. I was twenty years old and the idea of agreeing to such a vow was incomprehensible.

"It's a common problem," he continued, "and one that is supposed to be addressed by the teacher. It is well-recognized that as soon as a person awakens, she or he begins to pick up right where they left off with the previous enlightened body. Which nearly always means *teaching*. It is just what is familiar, almost like an instinct. The awakened mind seeks to awaken others. It is imperative that teachers apply the brakes to such a reflex. It is up to students to gain the experience that will allow them to understand how to translate the teachings so that they constitute a medicine that addresses the ills of the historical epoch in which they live."

I was trying to imagine how all this worked. "It seems so complex, too arbitrary," I said. "I mean, it can't just be a matter so many years, can it? Why thirty years? Why not just when the person is ready?"

"It's the way of the sudden enlightenment school," he replied matter-of-factly. "And you may as well start learning about it since it's the school you belong to."

FORTY
1977

I awoke in my bed, paralyzed.

I did not wake slowly—I was wide awake immediately and in an utter panic.

Not one muscle responded to command. Not even my eyelids. Laying on my back in my own bed, my eyes locked tight, I was completely immobilized.

But that was not the reason I was terrified.

Something horrifying was in my room. I could feel its presence just feet from the bed. It stood against the wall, off to my left, beside the bedroom door.

A dark shadow figure, hooded in a dark cape, it exuded an aura of supernatural menace.

The Soul Eater.

It did not occur to me to wonder how I could see it when I could not open my eyes. Where I lay and what I saw was many times more real than any previous experience, whether awake or dreaming. I was immersed in an ocean of psychic lushness, a thick stew of *intentions* that swirled everywhere, making all past experience seem like thin dishwater.

But none of those intentions approached the magnitude and intensity of the Soul Eater's. It was a heavy machete cutting through the overgrowth of human vines trailing hopes and wishes and desires. It was a great white shark of malevolence slicing through the teeming school of souls—and it had already picked me out of the multitude for its prey.

It was a deep and endless hunger about to devour the very nonphysical thing that made me, *me*.

And it was not alone.

Crouched beside it in the slanted light from the hallway, a gargoyle wrung its hands and swayed back and forth. It was the size of a large German shepherd and slavered like a Saint Bernard. Its interest in me was palpable—and wrenching. I stood in a kind of peril I had not ever experienced in this life. Yet it was a peril my soul recognized immediately from past encounters.

The Soul Eater and its gargoyle servant.

Dread figures out of the ancestral memory of humanity—not symbols, however, but living beings occupying a different kind of reality. Beings from the *nagual*.

I realized that one of two things had happened. Either I had somehow been pulled into the In-Between World in my sleep or else these *nagual* beings had the power to step into the *tonal*. Either way, my very immortality stood in dire jeopardy.

Completely cut off from my mortal body, my soul was boxed-in in the *nagual*, unable to twitch even the slightest of muscles. I struggled against bonds I could neither feel nor imagine. Everything was immobilized but my intent.

These thoughts passed through me at lightning speed, barely perceptible beneath the seething terror of imminent extinction. But upon recognizing the *nagual*, a poem emerged from the fog of awareness. It was one I had brought back with me from the other side of one of Robert Sharp's *presses*. Upon hearing it, Robert had pronounced it a *counter-spell* and had me commit it to memory—

> *like the eye*
> *of the hurricane*
> *i am: all change*
> *moves on without me*

No sooner than I had recited the last syllable than I was pulled along the hypotenuse of a triangle running perpendicular to the world of the five senses. Within the blink of a thought, I found myself in *The Center,* a previously unknown place of peace, harmony, and refuge. Yet it was a place utterly familiar to my soul: *Home.* Wrapped in light and warmth and loving-kindness, the panic passed and a sigh of deepest relief ushered me into the calm at the center of Creation. I was safe.

Something like time passed.

Certain that the spell had been broken, I exerted my intent to return to my body. It was somewhat like sending out a subtle wind ahead of the sail of awareness, a wind that would pull my life raft of identity along its appointed course.

I was back in my bedroom.

But I was not me.

I was sitting in my bed, swaying back and forth. The left side of my face was molten. Flaccid flesh sagged inches below my chin and drool hung from my drooping lip. No thought but one occupied my blissful mind: *to please my master.*

I was the gargoyle.

To my horror, I had been transformed into the mindless creature. I had reentered my body only to find it no longer my own—it had been possessed by the gargoyle and I was a stranger in the only physical form I remembered. Sharing the sensations of that debased creature was degrading in a way that only a spiritual violation of such magnitude could be: I was on the verge of being conjoined with the gargoyle forever.

My sense of identity was disintegrating and I was finding it almost impossible to concentrate. I was trapped inside a spiritual wasteland, falling further and further away from any recognizable landmark.

And to my great joy and pride, the Soul Eater was approaching from the left.

I was nearly snuffed out.

Desperate beyond measure, I cast about for the words to pull me *Home*—

> *like the eye*
> *of the hurricane*
> *i am: all change*
> *moves on without me*

I awoke the next morning shell-shocked. The bedroom looked the same. Leonor was just getting dressed to go downstairs and make break-fast for the children in shelter care.

"Did I wake you during the night?" I asked groggily.

"Anything unusual, weird dreams, or such?" I persisted when she shook her head *no*.

"No, nothing—why do you ask?" she replied.

The vividness of the experience was still with me—would be with me for years. I understood at that moment I had passed a test. But just barely.

"We need to go back to the Sierra, I answered.

She looked at me for an explanation.

"I need a teacher."

FORTY-ONE
1979

"When someone comes to me to be cured," Don Alfredo explained, "the first thing I ask them is, *Who has asked you for help that you refused?*"

I tried to logic it out myself, only asking questions if I simply could not make the leap in his reasoning.

"So guilt lies at the root of many illnesses?" I offered.

"That is part of it," he agreed. "But it goes deeper. The guilt becomes crystalized as a fear—a fear that the other person has cast a curse upon them. Or even worse, has gone to a *brujo* to have a grave curse laid upon them. This combination is like a seed that grows into an illness."

"How do you cure them, then?"

"Of course, their body-sickness must be addressed with herbs or other types of remedy. But I make it clear that their discomfort will not go away until the soul-sickness is cured by making amends with those they have offended. They may not be able to give what they were originally asked to, but they can offer to help in a way that really makes a difference. Their offer must be sincere and not just something to ease their conscience."

"That makes reconciliation possible in case the request was unreasonable or just wrong?"

He nodded. "Right and wrong are confusing because we never know the whole truth of what happened or what was really in people's heart when they acted. We only have the results of their actions to go by. My responsibility is not just to cure the person who comes to see me. My greater responsibility is to cure the community of anger that can grow into violence."

I knew this was a legitimate concern, as the Sierra was rife with stories about feuds that went on for generations. But there were even more stories about the evil eye and supernatural causes of misfortune.

"What if the offended person really did go to a brujo to have a curse cast on the person, Don Alfredo? What can you do then?"

He grimaced. "It is a very delicate matter. The person has paid the brujo, either with money or goods of some type. To simply remove the curse is to take away from the brujo's reputation, which results in conflict between him and me. And that disrupts the community even more. So I go personally to the brujo and tell him what I have done and that the person wishes to make amends, so the reason for the curse has been removed. Then I very respectfully ask him to remove the curse. I make him an offering of some food or tesguino. In this manner, his reputation is preserved and harmony can be restored to all concerned."

"So you have to make sure no one perceives you as taking sides, right? You have to remain neutral, no matter what?"

"No, Guillermo. I have to care for everyone with all my heart."

FORTY-TWO

1973

"I had a terrible fight in the *nagual* last night," explained Don Pancho, rubbing his bruised face.

We sat in the breezeway of the hotel. The heat of the day was hours away. The dew was just lifting from the sand. The morning smelled of salt air and breakfast.

Leonor and I had been running the hotel and restaurant on the San Blas beach for months before we learned that the caretaker, Don Pancho, was the town *curandero*. It wasn't something he or his wife, Aurelia, talked about at first. We had to ask, having noticed that he would break from his work and retreat to his room with the people who came to see him. He was an indigenous Cora, native to the Nayarit area, in his mid-seventies, who had been a curandero for fifty years. In the hierarchy of shamans, a "curer" like Don Pancho was one rung down from the more powerful *brujo*, or "witch," who could also cast spells of illness and misfortune.

"Two days ago, I removed the curse that a brujo in the jungle put on a young woman," he continued. "So last night, the brujo got his revenge. He called me to the Sierra, to the top of one of those columns growing up out of the canyon, to fight. There was no way to get down but to fall from such a terrible height. I could not escape and so just had to accept his beating me like a dog."

I stood and walked around behind him. I gently lifted his linen shirt. His back was covered in deep purple and black welts. His neck looked like he'd been choked.

"We all have a *nagual body*," he said, "but some people's will is so strong that their *nagual body* can affect your physical body through your *nagual body*."

"You have to be more careful, Don Pancho," I replied gently. "There are too many people depending on your help for you to take chances."

"It is very hard to refuse help to someone suffering," he said, half to himself. "I am an old man and cannot change. If I stop doing good to appease evil, how different will I be from evil?"

Aurelia came out with a couple plates of food and set them on the table in front of us.

"You see what I have to put up with?" she chided good-naturedly. "He can cure everyone but himself! What kind of old fool picks fights with witches?"

She pulled some forks out of her apron pocket and tossed them on the table in mock disgust. But she bent and kissed the top of his head tenderly before turning to go.

We ate in silence for a while, looking out on the ocean beyond the wide expanse of sand.

"The spirit world is just like this world," he said in between bites.

FORTY-THREE
1970

We Are I Am

The voice came like rolling thunder into my heart. I wept as I passed out, giving up the ghost to death.

I had spent a week up in the Sierra Nevada with some friends, camping by the river in King's Canyon, and returned with a strange fever from the many mosquito bites we'd all endured. Passing from chills to fever, over and over again, I exhausted myself trying to figure out what to do. It was the middle of the night, I had only recently returned from Tucson and had no one to call for company or support. I couldn't imagine it was too serious and so decided to just tough it out.

Dawn was still hours away when a different feeling overcame me. The cycle of fever and chills took its toll and it seemed like I was expelling my life force into the sweat-soaked bedclothes. I became convinced I was dying. My conscious awareness retreated. I was about to pass out. It seemed like the natural course of events. The cloudiness of anxiety and confusion lifted. I could see myself turning away from this world and stepping into the next. I could hear the voice welcoming me as I passed out.

We Are I Am

I was surprised the next morning. I was not expecting to wake up. My memory of the previous night was crystal clear. My thoughts were a river held back by a dam. A dam that was at the bursting point.

I stood, walked over to my desk and sat down in front of a pad of paper. I could see the whole page behind my eyes before writing a single word. It all came out in a single uninterrupted flow—

There is One Heaven and One Earth

One Soul and One Body
One Seed and One Tree

There is One Unseen and One Seen
One Silence and One Song
One Essence and One Reflection

There is One Origin and nothing else
In the end what is left but Soul?
And what is Soul but Seed?
And what is Seed but Origin?

And what is Life but the eternal revelation of this Origin?
And what is Truth but the eternal realization of this Origin?

Origin means Return
Origin means that there is One Life
What is Love but the manifestation of this Origin?
Origin means that there is One Soul

What is Seed but Essence, and the eternal embodiment of Essence?
What is Soul but the Mist, and the eternal communion of this Mist?
And what is the Mist but the One Love?

Origin means Family
Family means Home
Home means Return to Essence

Each of these words carried so much emotional significance that I felt myself back in the midst of the experience, weeping with joy and relief. The entire litany of names seemed to be an extension, an illumination, of the saying, *We Are I Am.*

Socrates said "Death is the Great Teacher." There are ancient traditions that encourage us to imagine ourselves on our deathbed in order to let slip the body from our anxious grasp. Other modern observers like to say that we ought to hold death close and use it as an advisor. In my experience, taking death seriously, going forward to meet it instead of running from it, is an opening of the soul to the World Soul. An opening of the mind to the One Mind. Freed of bodily concerns and personal memories, the heart opens to an *inflowing* of understanding that transforms one's life in relation to the One Life. It is not a matter of knowledge or an understanding of things—rather, it is an immediate grasp of the essential relationships *between* things.

I would not suggest that my personal revelation carries any meaning for others but I would suggest that everyone's personal revelation lies just across the border between the physical body and the spiritual body.

FORTY-FOUR
1973

This is a brujo, I realized through the haze of morphine.

"It's a miracle," whispered Aurelia. "He never comes here this time of year."

Don Pancho turned to me and said, "This is the only man I know of who can save your life."

Leonor squeezed my hand hopefully. Just the day before she'd been told that the amoebic dysentery was killing me and she needed to begin making arrangements for my burial.

He walked across the restaurant and took my hand in his, feeling my pulse. His physical presence was extraordinary, exerting a kind of gravity unlike anyone I had ever met. *This is a brujo!*

No one knew his real name. He had disappeared into his own myth years ago, becoming *King of the Shadows,* the one who walks with the souls of the land. I never saw his face. I looked at it a thousand times but could never see it. He cast a cloud of shadows around himself, made himself invisible, pushed people away. It was like coming across a jaguar in the rain forest. It was there one moment and the next moment you doubted it had ever been there.

"I cannot help you if you are afraid of dying," he growled. His voice was like gravel in a blender.

"I have been living among shadows for days," I mumbled. "They comfort me." I learned later that he considered this a good omen since I had not yet heard his name spoken.

He withdrew to his battered old pickup and returned with four bags of herbs, which he handed to Leonor. "Boil all of these together in a big pot. Give him a cup of its tea and take him to bed immediately. Strain off the rest and place it in the refrigerator. He must have a cup three times a day for a week. Nothing else or it will kill him. For another week, he must drink only lemon water. Nothing else or it will kill him. Then soups and soft food for a while until he regains his strength."

That was that. He went to the refrigerator, pulled out a bottle of beer and went off to a corner to talk with Don Pancho about things such beings talk about in private.

I had not eaten anything but water for a week. My intestines had convulsed so much that all I had left to excrete was blood. I had not been out of bed for many days but I awoke in bed, alone in our room, and got up to go looking for Leonor. The three of them could not believe their eyes when I had stepped into the kitchen, soaking wet with perspiration from the effort of walking fifty feet.

Five minutes later, the door at the opposite end of the restaurant had opened and in had stepped King of the Shadows. He had never before come to San Blas in the summer—it wasn't the right time to collect the medicines he usually harvested from the surrounding jungle.

I gulped down the cup of tea Leonor handed me. Even so, I could barely finish it, so powerful was its effect. I had to be helped back to the room and was asleep before getting to the bed.

I awoke the next morning, some eighteen hours later, fully refreshed and feeling absolutely normal. Amazed that all the pain and symptoms had disappeared, I dressed and headed toward the kitchen. Within twenty steps, I realized that all had not returned to normal. By the time I reached the kitchen, I was exhausted, panting and sweating. As I was to discover, it would be two years before my endurance returned to anything like normal.

I kept to the regimen King of the Shadows demanded. My condition improved. As there was no more pain, I quit taking the morphine, so the world came back into focus and I regained my concentration. Since I was pretty much confined to the hotel, I began spending most of my time with King of the Shadows. I would rise early and have breakfast with him, listening to him detail the places he was going that day and the medicines he was looking for. The rest of the day, I rested and played chess and waited for him to return. We would eat the afternoon meal and relive the day's work before everything came to a standstill for siesta time. The evening and night were the goldmine for me. I would sit in his room while he brought in all that he'd collected that day and undertake the laborious task of stripping bark or leaves or whatever part of the plant he knew to be beneficial.

"You should leave him alone, Guillermo," Don Pancho admonished me one day as I was following King of the Shadows out of the restaurant. "He doesn't like company."

"Now, now, Panchito," he replied over his shoulder. "He called me here! I need to find out why!"

The mess he made of his room every night was legendary. Piles of branches and leaves a meter deep in every corner. But the girls who came to clean the rooms every morning never complained. He cured them of several vexing discomforts that they could not divulge to their local doctors.

"They call this plant such-and-such here in San Blas," he would tell me, "but in Oaxaca it is known as this-or-that. You cannot remove it from the trunk during such-and-such phase of the moon and you must speak to it in this-or-that manner. It is good for curing such-and-such in the elderly and, if prepared in this-or-that manner, will cause such-and-such illness in young men." Such was the common formula of his description of each plant. But he nearly always had stories about this or that mishap or unexpected outcome of a treatment related to each. Like most indigenous people I've spent time with, he had a ribald sense of humor that picked at the scabs of human nature—sex, jealousy, envy, gossip, revenge, and so forth, all formed part of his commentary on the ironies and absurdities of life.

One day he did not return for the afternoon meal. Or siesta. Or breakfast the next morning.

"Don't worry," Don Pancho told me. "It's the rest of the jungle that has to be careful of him." He squinted at me for emphasis. "*You* need to be careful of him. He is a powerful *nagual* and no one can ever predict what he will do next."

I understood what he meant. A sense of barely contained danger accompanied the brujo wherever he went. Everyone I talked to had stories of seeing him shape-shift into an owl or ocelot. They all agreed he was several hundred years old and able to cause as much ill as good. A village in the south had to be abandoned, a common story went, after he poisoned its well with a single word.

A pounding on my door woke me from my siesta. It was King of the Shadows, caked in dust and spider webs and bits of twigs and leaf litter.

"So, now I know," he crowed, shaking my hand formally. "Thank you for calling me."

I returned his handshake respectfully. I try never to contradict my teachers or expose my ignorance unnecessarily. I figure they are talking about something that I will understand when the time is right, so I keep my silence whenever possible. And wait. Such people have their own way of communicating and interrupting them with questions about *what I want to know* often keeps them from telling me *what they want me to know.*

"I was wandering far from any path, praying to the jungle for a sign. One of those feathered serpents they have around here fell from a tree right in front of me. I knew how partial you are to snakes. And that you came from far away. So I recognized the feathered serpent as your *nahualli*, your animal spirit, and followed it."

I had not seen the famous feathered snakes of San Blas but had heard about them a lot—they had tufts of feathers on their heads, it was said. They had the odd habit of dropping from trees, especially irritating to women washing their clothes in the river, since mud splashed all over their drying clothes. They were said to be two or three meters long and as thick as a man's calf or even thigh. From what I had gathered, they were a kind of large boa constrictor. Their habit of dropping from trees gave the impression of flying, hence their "feathered" or "winged" aspect. My rational conjecture aside, however, the locals had all *seen* their feathered crests.

"It led me to a burrow in the side of a hill. It crawled into the burrow and I followed it. But the tunnel was for a small animal, so I had to dig it out as I went. That took me all night because it extended nearly straight back into the hill for perhaps four meters. As I got close to the end, the feathered serpent lay coiled, sleeping comfortably and ignoring me."

He made a show of brushing the dirt from his shirt and pants. "I was pretty tired by that time and so rolled over onto my back in order to sleep myself. Looking up like that, you'll never guess what I saw. There, directly above the feathered snake, growing down through the roof of the burrow, was a golden root."

My reaction was not as enthused as he had anticipated.

"The golden root is the queen of all medicines. It cures every man-made disease in the world. Even the smallest dose restores an adult to full health. A medium dose restores the terminally ill to full vitality. A full dose pulls those who have been dead for only a few hours back into the land of the living. It is the magical root of longevity. The panacea."

I smiled widely. "And you *found* it?"

He unbuttoned his shirt and drew out a damp towel. Unfolding it, he exposed a root about two feet long that was, indeed, of a rich gold color. More extraordinary, however, was the fact that it was in the form of a woman.

"It took me most of the day today to remove it from the ground. You must dig around it in a way that does not ever injure it or it will not come with you. So I had to lie on my back, sharing the burrow with the feathered snake, slowly carving the soil away from the golden root."

He sighed. "They do not put anything but the thinnest little vine with just a few small leaves above ground. On the rainforest floor, their little vines are impossible to find. I have been searching for the golden root for more than thirty years. If not for your animal companion, I never would have found it."

"You saved my life," I replied.

"Now we are even," he said.

Our *nagual-pact* fulfilled, King of the Shadows gathered up all his gear and headed off to his next stop on the medicine road.

FORTY-FIVE
1985

It was time to say my goodbyes to the rain forest.

I'd been staying in Palenque for two months, spending as much time wandering the lush jungle around the famous archaeological site as the ruins themselves. The opportunity to roam unimpeded among the sprawling buttresses of the giant strangler figs, delicate fountains of flowering bromeliads, and teeming superabundance of wildlife had been one of the most sustained mystical experiences of my life. The tropical lowland, I had found, is the high desert turned inside-out.

The day had come to say goodbye. Goodbye to the leaf-cutter ants, with whom I had spent innumerable hours watching their streaming battalions gathering the leaves that allowed them to farm the fungus upon which the entire colony depended. Goodbye to the giant hermit hummingbird, with its curious habit of rushing up on unsuspecting trekkers and hovering mere inches from their face like the doe-eyed fairies of yore. And goodbye to the elusive howler monkeys that I had tried futilely to track by the sound of their raucous calls echoing among the hills and rills of the jungle.

I stepped off the trail and into the forest with a clear destination in mind: there was a clearing not too far from the Princess' Bath—a deep place in the stream running out of the ruins above, once reserved as the bathing-place of a Mayan princess of old—where the howlers sometimes left their juveniles to frolic under the supervision of a single, beleaguered, adult while they went off to forage. I was looking forward to spending a few hours in the shade of one of the strangler figs, watching the young monkeys leaping among the canopy as they sparred with each other and relentlessly teased the poor adult left in charge of the nursery.

But no sooner had I entered the deep shadows of the rain forest than the distant roar of a howler ricocheted through the rolling hills. My ears picked up immediately—what a fortuitous sign, one last opportunity to track the elusive monkey by its intermittent howls. I set off in the direction of its echoes, knowing from experience that this wasn't necessarily the best strategy. The problem was that the great trees and limestone hills created a maze through which the echoes bounced maddeningly, making it all but impossible to determine the actual location of the call. If that wasn't complicated enough, I'd found that I had to make the best time possible since the howlers only called for so long before falling silent again.

The calls kept coming, though, drawing me off into a part of the forest I hadn't investigated before. Skirting the occasional hillock and shallow ravine, I was rewarded by hearing the howler calling from just the other side of a particularly lush ridge of fern-covered boulders. I stopped in my tracks, waiting to catch one more call to pinpoint the monkey's whereabouts—but of course, that was precisely when the howler stopped calling. It seemed my approach had not gone unobserved.

I settled in for a few minutes, scanning the area closely. After determining it couldn't be seen in the canopy above, I searched for hiding places on the ground. The boulders I crouched behind formed part of the bank of a shallow stream that was about fifteen feet across. The water was crystal clear, just a few inches deep, flowing over the glossy surface of the limestone bed. Just upstream a few dozen feet stood a waterfall about twenty feet tall made of the same limestone. Clearly the floor of the jungle had long ago dropped some twenty feet, exposing this ice-green cliff. The gentle stream washed over the single block of limestone, following the timeworn channels coated with slippery moss.

Suddenly, I heard it. Up above, on the top of the waterfall: the definite sound of splashing! I could picture the howler crouched beside a shallow pool in the limestone, playing with the water as it drank its fill.

I was elated. After so many efforts, I had successfully tracked a wild monkey through the virgin rain forest. I had never felt so much a part of nature, so in sync with its mysterious ways. I was beaming, half to myself and half to the world around me, as I made my way down the embankment, determined to lay eyes on the howler before it returned to the canopy.

Never before nor since have I moved so stealthily. The humidity kept the vegetation from drying out, so my steps were muffled as long as I avoided overturning a stone. Crossing the stream, I scanned the waterfall for the best route to the top and spotted a more ragged face of the stone offering a series of dry handholds and footholds. It was only twenty feet tall, but I crept up as though it were a thousand-foot precipice—not because I was concerned about falling but for fear of alerting the howler to my presence.

I reached the top. The next handhold was going to raise my eyes above the lip of the waterfall. The splashing had grown louder and even more vigorous, leading me to hope that the monkey was so distracted playing that it might fail to notice me for a few seconds. I took a deep breath and paused before moving, considering my alternatives. If I moved slowly, the howler might spot the movement and take off before I actually got to see it—if I moved quickly, it might startle it where a slower movement might have afforded a longer view. The deciding factor was my hat, a dull green broad-brimmed affair that might not be so recognizable to a monkey as the contour of a naked head. The splashing just above me grew so spirited that I was being doused by water drops where I hung. It was the moment of truth. I decided on moving quickly.

I raised my head above the edge of the waterfall.

It was not a howler monkey.

There, not three feet from me, splashing madly in the act of bathing, was a huge black eagle.

Indeed, so enraptured with dunking itself in the water and throwing water on its back with its wings was it, that its eyes were clouded by its nictitating membrane protecting it from the water. It was a full ten seconds before it was aware of me.

In that ten seconds I passed through a world of awe: from deeply shocked at coming face-to-face with the eagle, to wonderstruck at its size and grandeur, to humbled at being present at a moment that nature generally holds secret.

That ten seconds of bliss passed and pure chaos ensued. The eagle's eyes cleared and it saw me a mere wing's length in front of it, pulled up to it full height of nearly three feet, let out a scream that echoes in my mind to this day, exploded out of the pool, spread its broad wings wide, and leapt over my head so close that its talons brushed the top of my hat. I turned as best I could to follow its flight, which consisted of that one short hop over me to glide over to a tree branch some seventy-five feet away. It closed its wings on landing and raised its crest—in alarm or as a threat, I could not say. But I felt decidedly vulnerable at the moment, clinging to the edge of the waterfall like that while trying to look behind me. I pulled myself up quickly and turned to sit facing the eagle, my legs dangling over the edge and my butt sitting in an inch of water.

We sat on our respective perches staring at one another, both of us, it seemed, calming a bit as the adrenaline stopped pumping. For its part, the eagle eventually started preening, which it would do normally after a bath, shaking off the water, running feathers through its beak, and scratching ecstatically with its great talons. For my part, I scooted nonchalantly to a drier place on the waterfall and fell into a deep reverie watching the magnificent creature at home in its domain. As its feathers dried, I could see it wasn't exactly black but a very dark grey color with some white on it tail. It occasionally interrupted its preening to peer closely at something moving on the ground but lost interest quickly in favor of continued pluming. I entered *eagle time,* a long unbroken moment of total focus on one spatial act at a time. It was precisely the same type of concentration that opens the gate to the *nagual.* There is a part of me sitting there across from that eagle still.

At some point, I noticed the shadows lengthening and realized it was time to make my way back to the world of hostels and buses and airplanes. I stood and stretched. The eagle bowed and stretched. I moved off toward the embankment. The eagle opened its wings and dropped out of the tree, gliding off into the shadows of the next ravine.

I had come to say farewell to the rain forest that had welcomed me with open arms.

It was the best farewell party I ever had.

FORTY-SIX
1974

"I like you, I really do," said the program manager of the group homes. "But you're just too young for me to hire you as house parents. Some of the boys are just a few years younger than you. And your wife is expecting in six months. It's just too risky."

"I understand," I replied, standing to go. "Thanks for considering it."

"Like I say, I like you," he repeated, shuffling through my application packet. He paused to read a page.

"This letter of recommendation written by Harry Green," he said. "That's not the same Harry Green who was the radio host in Boulder, is it?"

I nodded yes.

"I used to listen to him all the time. He had an amazing mind." He re-read the letter.

"This is quite a recommendation," he said.

That is how we got the job running the group home for troubled boys, which led to our running the shelter home for abused and neglected children, which led to designing and administering social service programs for at-risk families—all of which allowed us to be well used by life for the next twenty years.

The *interconnectedness of all things,* I was learning, is not an abstract concept.

FORTY-SEVEN
1987

"They say I went Abbo," said Wayne, smiling broad as his broad-brimmed leather hat.

"They mean it to be derogatory, like it's bad to emulate the Aborigine way," explained Lindy, "but he takes it as a measure of his success."

"They don't get how empty their lives are, just drinking and pubbing when they've got this treasure of wisdom and art all around." Wayne spread his arms wide, sweeping all the Outback into a single pass of adoration.

We sat in the shade of a great ghost gum, our campers parked some fifty feet from the edge of the billabong. Dusk was approaching and we were enjoying the conversation of new friends accompanied by the smell of dinner cooking on the campfire.

It had been a full day. We'd met Wayne and Lindy at the entrance of one of the ancient walls of Aboriginal rock art. Lindy, seven months pregnant, was climbing down from their pickup and Leonor had stepped closer to give her an arm of support. That's all it took. Wayne had immediately offered to decipher the hallucinogenic paintings for us, an act of generosity that translated the vision of Dreamtime and the ancestors and mimi spirits into a living tapestry of mythic truth. Kakadu National Park is world-famous for its many rock art sites and Wayne had been eager to expose us to several of the most awe-inspiring. Despite the heat of the day, we had traveled around between sites until mid-afternoon, when we stopped our little two-camper caravan for a picnic lunch.

"How about a quick bath, mate?" Wayne had asked innocently enough.

I looked at him with one eyebrow raised skeptically.

"No worries—you watch my back and I'll watch yours," he smiled reassuringly.

We headed off to a series of channels, towels and soap in hand.

"The water's clear," he said as we stood on the bank, "so you can see a croc coming and give me a holler in time for me to climb out." He stripped down to his shorts and stepped into the water before I could answer.

The recklessness of the situation was not lost on me. The saltwater crocodiles of Kakadu are enormous and responsible for numerous deaths every year. In the week we'd been there, three tourists had been killed by crocodiles. I knew, too, that just climbing out of the water wasn't enough—the crocs were able to propel themselves yards out of the water to take prey too close to the edge.

I was keyed up, straining to peer into the water as far away as possible. Wayne played it nonchalant but he didn't stay in the water any longer than he had to.

"All right, mate, have a go," he exclaimed enthusiastically.

If I was keyed up before, I don't know what I was then, neck-deep in the crystal water, lathering up and rinsing off as quickly as I could without splashing around like a wounded animal. It was nerve-racking in the extreme—every shadow of a ripple on the channel floor sent a rush of adrenaline through me. It wasn't made any more comforting by the fact that Wayne would periodically start whistling carelessly and pretend to look off at clouds in the sky. His lightness only accented the gravity of the moment: I was transported thousands of years backwards, placed on an equal footing with all of nature—not the dominant species but the fragile prey of prehistoric goliaths. Treading water where twenty-foot monsters glided along like death incarnate, I was terrified on an instinctual level untouched by rational thought.

But climbing out of the water, I was exhilarated. My skin felt brand new in the sun, as if by outliving my terror I had shed an old skin. My awareness seemed to extend yards beyond my body, as if I could have sensed a crocodile approaching by myself. I was drunk on light, outside myself, ecstatic, the miracle of being alive all I could perceive.

"You've been baptized, mate." I looked into his pale blue eyes as he dried his long blonde hair. He had, indeed, gone Abbo.

It had been a full day. We'd driven miles off any road to arrive at this secret billabong ringed by ghost gums. The sun hung on one horizon as the full moon rose on the other. A sense of balance and rightness charged the air. Things seemed to be in their place. Birds sang the sun to sleep. Crickets summoned the moon to wake within the crystal ball of the sky. Out bellies were full, our minds were empty.

Lindy reached inside their camper, pulled out a didgeridoo, and handed it to Wayne. "It always sounds so wonderful around a campfire," she told him.

He took the instrument, by tradition a long branch hollowed out by termites, and began to play in that strange unending breath that turns the musician into air itself. He played the song of the dingo and the song of the owl and the song of the wallaby and the song of the kookaburra. I added wood to the fire and Wayne played the song of the haunted night and the ghost herons hidden in the rushes around the billabong wailed like lost souls.

The moon rose high overhead and a long line of flying foxes made their way across its face, their outlines silhouetted in memory forever. The sound of the didgeridoo spilled out into the dark, echoed off the moon's reflection in the still surface of the billabong, and helped organize the stars into constellations.

Eventually the song faded away, following the dying fire back to that common source from which they both sprang. We were already dreaming as we bade goodnight and headed for bed.

I was awakened by the singing of a crocodile. Somewhere between growling and bellowing, the sound drew me out of bed and into the dead of night. A slight chill crept off the billabong. The moon had set. The stars were closer than I had ever seen them in my life. The Southern Cross drove home the point that I was not looking at the sky I knew.

It was a moment out of time. The crocodile's song was answered from far away in the night, like an echo from the time of the dinosaurs. Insects chirruped shyly. Occasional splashes from the dark lagoon signaled the unsleeping transformation of energy up the food chain. The land sighed and its breath lay close to the ground, a silver mist the color of the stars. The world, it seemed, had waited forever for just this moment.

Something very big burst through Earth's upper atmosphere. A massive meteor sailed a straight line trajectory across the sky, immune to Earth's gravity. Dripping molten orange, green, and blue in its wake, the fiery meteor seared the flesh of night. It did not fall like a meteorite and burn up on its plunge toward Earth. It shot instead straight across the atmosphere, burning off just a small portion of its mass in the briefest display of celestial pyrotechnics. And it burst back out through the other side of Earth's atmosphere, disappearing back into frictionless space.

Five seconds, perhaps ten seconds, and it was gone as silently as it had arrived.

But it left me in its wake: standing on the edge of the universe, I was suddenly adrift in the sea of stars where I had always felt I stood on firm ground.

"There's a corroboree this evening," Wayne announced over breakfast. "It features the most famous Aboriginal didgeridoo player alive—he's a living legend. I've hoped to see him perform for years but never been in the right place at the right time. He's getting on in age and there might not be another chance like this."

We nodded agreeably. After all, he hadn't steered us anywhere but right so far.

"The only thing is, it's at a big tourist resort out in the middle of nowhere. About two hundred miles away, so we'd have some driving to do." You could hear in his voice that the driving was nothing compared to having to visit a commercial resort.

We left early but still arrived late—it was further than he'd thought and we were approaching from the wrong side, where no paved road existed. The performance was nearly over by the time we got seated in the very back of the large audience. A couple hundred folding chairs had been set up outdoors around a makeshift stage.

But the big finale was just getting started. The music was both electrifying and hypnotic, the long droning of the didgeridoo accompanied by click sticks and drums setting the dreamlike atmosphere for the singers and dancers. The men were all painted in strange symbols with white paint that seemed alive when they moved, acting out a grand creation story that involved mimicking the ways of various animals and spirits. This magnificent spectacle lasted nearly a half-hour and was a joy to behold.

The star of the show was the old man Wayne had come to hear. His didgeridoo did not just sing—it painted cave art images in the air. He was obviously held in high esteem by the rest of the musicians and dancers. His bearing bespoke a wise and dignified life.

As the applause died down, the old man took to the microphone and asked everyone who wanted to learn the didgeridoo to come up on the stage and try it out. This was obviously part of the show, geared to the tourist audience, but the old man's warmth and good nature made it seem natural. Several folks from the audience came forward and he demonstrated how to purse one's lips and blow into the didgeridoo somewhat like a trombone. Everyone tried their best but made the kind of farting sounds that sent the rest of the audience into laughter.

"No one else, then?" asked the old man. "Come on now, don't be shy."

Lindy pushed Wayne out of his chair hard enough that he had to stand or fall.

"There we go," the old man called out. "The young fella in the back!"

Wayne reached the stage and, instead of simply taking the didgeridoo offered him, extended his hand to the old man with obvious respect. The old man took his hand and shook it like an old friend, then handed over the didgeridoo.

Before he could give any instructions, Wayne began playing.

The old man stepped back in surprise and, smiling with delight, called out to the rest of the musicians, "Hit it boys!" The percussionists all set up a beat and the old man took up his didgeridoo and began playing, weaving around Wayne's drone. That began a duet that lasted fifteen minutes, where the two didgeridoos took turns leading and following, calling and responding, mimicking each others' dingo barks and kook-aburra calls, and just generally setting the night on fire.

The old man was clearly having fun. Wayne was just as clearly playing his heart out, keeping up his end of a duet with his longtime hero. The audience, which had been standing and preparing to leave, settled back into their chairs, realizing that something special was happening on the stage. I glanced at Lindy and was not surprised to see her crying—I felt a lump in my throat, as well.

The song wound down, the droning of the two didgeridoos holding the last of it in a fading pulse, a dying ember, a passing rainstorm. So soft the ending, it just flowed into silence as easy as a river flowing into the sea.

The old man set down his didgeridoo and hugged Wayne, hugged him in a long, genuine show of affection. Wayne nodded and grinned at what the old man was saying in his ear.

It was suddenly Christmas and I was happier seeing someone else opening their gift than I was opening my own.

FORTY-EIGHT

1972

"Thirty years," repeated Master Khigh Alx Dhiegh. "Think carefully before speaking."

I was twenty-two years old and my teacher was ready to terminate my apprenticeship. After two years of concentrated study, he had decided the time had come to initiate me into the sudden enlightenment school. All he required of me was my vow to neither teach nor divulge any of what I'd learned until at least thirty years had passed. He was taking the vow very seriously, so I knew I needed to as well. But I was twenty-two years old and I could not imagine ever wanting to teach. If it was a serious matter to Master Khigh, though, then it had to be a serious matter to me.

I took a deep breath. "I do solemnly vow to refrain from teaching for thirty years. I do solemnly vow to refrain from divulging what I have learned for thirty years. I do solemnly vow to continue these teachings accurately when my silence is broken."

Master Khigh smiled proudly. His eyes seemed to be watering in the candlelight. He picked up the bell beside the candle and rang it softly. He set it back down on the yellow prayer flag between us and spoke formally.

"I have taught you everything I know, just as my teacher taught me everything he knew. After tonight, you will be as qualified to teach as I am. And, just as I carried my teacher's knowledge further into the next generation, you will carry my knowledge further into the coming generation.

"After tonight, we will no longer meet as teacher and student because your formal studies in divination have come to an end. Now you must go out into the world and learn about human nature. Our school encourages independence, autonomy and self-sufficiency, not dependence on a teacher. To be a diviner, you must take the step beyond learning. You must serve others. Only in this way will you come to embody the Oracle."

Now I felt my eyes watering. He was sending me away. My life was about to change completely.

He picked up the bell again and rang it more loudly.

"These are the words with which my teacher initiated me and I repeat them in the act of initiating you."

Spreading his arms wide with palms facing up, he recited a traditional formula—

> *In the oneness of time, there is only this generation.*
> *The first enlightened being had no predecessor.*
> *No teacher.*
> *No teaching.*
> *No model.*
> *No preconception.*
> *This is worthy of deep reflection.*
>
> *In the oneness of time, you are the first enlightened being.*
> *Without predecessor.*
> *Without teacher.*
> *Without teaching.*
> *Without model.*
> *Without preconception.*
> *Alive and Aware Space.*
> *An awake omnipresence between and around and within all things*
>   *and all beings.*
> *The Way encompassing all making up the All.*
>
> *Now, what shall you do with this initiated body?*

FORTY-NINE
1977

"I hate you," spat the teenage girl angrily.

Her companion, a year younger, sobbed, "We shouldn't be here."

It was two in the morning and the police had just dropped the girls off at the shelter home. I'd gotten a call earlier waking me and letting me know they were arriving. And letting me know they were upset.

"I know," I replied. "I can't believe this is happening to you. I am so sorry."

They calmed just a little, sensing they might have an ally. It was my role to provide a safe place for the children, ensuring that they were not further traumatized by the crisis. For crisis it was: uprooted from all routine, taken by law enforcement to a strange place, unable to speak to family—for anyone of any age, these circumstances would trigger the deepest fears. The first minutes at the shelter home needed to set a tone of normalcy for the children.

"Then we can call our parents and have them pick us up?" the older girl said hopefully. The younger one brightened a bit at this thought.

"First thing in the morning," I said reassuringly, "we'll have a meeting with your parents and then everything will get straightened out."

"This whole thing is all a big lie," said the younger girl, wringing her hands.

From the phone call I knew that the girls lived in the dorm of a Christian boarding school in one of the smaller towns about forty minutes to the south. They were overheard by a third girl talking about how they were both being sexually abused by their fathers whenever they went home. The third girl had told a teacher, who immediately called child protective services, who immediately called the police, who immediately picked the girls up and brought them to the shelter home. I knew from the phone call that they were denying they had the conversation. And were denying any abuse.

"I have to tell you that mistakes happen sometimes. You know how serious adults get when there's a worry about children's safety. You shouldn't worry. Your folks are going to straighten everything out in the morning."

"Why are we being punished?" the older girl demanded.

"Let me show you something, girls," I replied, standing and opening the door to the office. I led them out past the front door and took the long way around, through the living room with video games on the floor, through the sliding wood doors into the dining room that seated a dozen, through the old-fashioned pantry, past the downstairs bathroom with its antique eagle-claw tub, and back to a bedroom next to the office. I opened the door softly and let the hall light shine in enough that they could see a couple of six- and seven-year-old girls sleeping in their beds.

I motioned them to follow me upstairs. The stairs of the hundred-year-old house squeaked but no one minded it after a while. "This is my wife's and my room," I whispered. "That's the boys' room, that's the girls' room, and this is my daughter's room." I opened the door quietly and took the girls in.

My daughter sat up in bed. "Is everything okay?" she whispered, not wanting to wake the one-year-old baby in the crib beside her bed.

"Just showing them around," I whispered back.

"Hi," she said. She was about their age.

"Hi," they returned her little wave.

The baby turned in its sleep.

"And that's the upstairs bathroom with a shower," I continued, as if I were really just showing them the house.

Back in the hallway, I stopped outside the girls' bedroom.

"Is that your baby?" the younger girl asked.

"No, he's here because his parents mistreated him," I replied.

There weren't any other girls in their room at the moment, so I flipped the light on. Two sets of bunk beds and a large dresser pretty much filled the small room.

I opened the closet door and pointed to the rows of hooks on the wall. "There's clean nightgowns and robes hanging there. You are free to use them if you like."

"What time will the meeting be in the morning?" the older girl asked.

"Nine o'clock, as soon as the offices across the street open. I'll wake you in plenty of time to get ready. Now try not to worry about things and just get some sleep."

I turned, closing the door behind me.

"Thank you," they said nearly in unison.

"I need for you to bring the girls all the way back to my office," the juvenile court director told me over the phone. "It's going to be a real circus. Both sets of parents, the minister and bigwigs from their congregation. Once you get here, find a corner and stay put. Hard to say how this is going to go."

I walked the girls over to the courthouse and through the maze of offices to the director's. There were voices to be heard through his closed door. I knocked and ushered the girls into the room.

No sooner had they entered than their parents, the minister and others started yelling angrily, "Why are you lying about this? How could you! Look at the trouble you've caused! What were you thinking? Your poor parents! You should be ashamed!" It was like a nightmarish Greek chorus.

Ordinarily, the director wouldn't allow this kind of behavior in his office. But he had talked to the school principal and knew something about these two girls. He sat back in his chair and allowed events to unfold.

A full minute of this yelling and the adults showed no sign of having to catch their breath.

The older girl suddenly yelled over the top of them, "We came in here ready to lie for you!"

The silence was damning.

The younger girl turned to me and said, "Take us home."

They stayed with us for a couple months, testing this foster home and that until they found one they felt comfortable in. They never saw their parents again.

•

Over the course of the following fifteen years, we lived with more than two thousand abused and neglected children. During that time, I often thought about Master Khigh telling me to go out into the world and experience the light and shadow sides of human nature. The heart, as I learned repeatedly, can reverse itself instantaneously.

FIFTY

1972

"No!" exclaimed Ralphie, flailing at a retreating Richard.

I picked up a quarter of the peanut butter sandwich and handed it to Richard, who smelled it carefully before taking a cautious bite.

Ralphie displayed his displeasure by rocking vigorously on the picnic bench, his hands clenched tightly in his lap.

"Shhh," I reassured him, patting him lightly on his back. It was like touching stone. His musculature was locked in nearly perpetual spasm.

They were cousins, both six years old, and polar opposites. Ralphie was dark-haired, dark-eyed, and aggressive. Richard was blonde, blue-eyed, and passive. What they had in common was their autism.

And a nightmarish past.

Ralphie's mother was already tired of taking care of one kid when her sister showed up one day and dropped Richard off for a couple hours—and never came back. As soon as the boys could crawl, she'd put their mattresses in the basement and then locked them in there until the day they were discovered by a pair of social workers. What they found shocked even their world-weary sensibilities.

The basement reeked of feces and rot. They had to step over a large pile of molding food at the bottom of the stairs. The basement was in near total darkness—they had to take a light bulb from a fixture in the house and screw it into the empty socket in the ceiling. When the light came on, two naked children cowered on their bare, filthy, mattresses. They were five years old at that time and hadn't seen light, except for the times Ralphie's mother opened the door at the top of the stairs to throw food down, for at least three years.

They led Richard out by wrapping him in a blanket and covering his eyes. Ralphie had to be sedated after biting and scratching everyone who tried to touch him.

Richard had never uttered a sound except for a nasal whine when distressed. Ralphie had a vocabulary of one word, which was always yelled and accompanied by a flailing fist. Richard would sit for hours, staring blankly off into some inner world while slapping the fingertips of his hands together with remarkable dexterity. Ralphie would sit cross-legged, rocking back and forth and glaring angrily at the floor in front of him. When he wanted to move, he would scoot along on his haunches with legs crossed. He could only walk when an adult held his hand and even then he walked terribly bow-legged.

I met the boys a year later when I took a job at a private ranch for children with developmental disabilities. They had adapted well to their new surroundings, which must have seemed like paradise to them. The home was residence to fifteen children and had a special education teacher assigned by the state. It sat on several acres at the base of the Santa Susana Knolls, which were likewise home to five spectacularly grand California Live Oaks. Tame peacocks roamed the grounds, wailing plaintively for something they lost long ago.

After dinner every evening, the home fell into a fixed routine. All the children sat around the television while caregivers took them one-by-one for a bath. One of the women took the girls, of course, and I took the boys. After bathing them, they were dressed in pajamas and a robe and returned to the living room to watch some more television before bedtime.

One evening, after dressing Richard in his pajamas, I feigned exasperation, exclaiming, "Oh, I forgot your bathrobe! Come on, let's go find it." Taking his hand, we marched back to boys' dorm, where I sat him on his bed while I pretended to look for his robe.

"Hmmpff!" I grunted. "Where'd I leave it? You stay here a minute, Richard, I'll be right back." With that, I exited down the hall, took a side door outside, and circled back to see what Richard was doing.

Out of safety concerns, the children were never unsupervised, so this was the first time since his rescue that he was experiencing the sense of being by himself.

He sat on the end of the bed, slapping his fingertips together and gazing off into his own world. But after a few minutes, he started looking around attentively—something I had never seen him do before. He was actually taking in his surroundings rather than withdrawing from them. He stood and then walked slowly on tiptoe to his dresser. Carefully opening the bottom drawer, he picked out a pair of pants with one hand and flung them over his head onto the floor. With the other hand, he did the same to another pair of pants. And so on, with each item in the drawer. Carefully closing that drawer, he just as carefully opened the one above it. One by one, he worked his way ambidextrously through all his shirts, flinging them overhead where they floated to the floor. And then it was the top drawer's turn, where every t-shirt and pair of underwear and socks met a similar fate.

He managed to empty out his dresser in just a couple of minutes. But it was the only truly animated period of time he had exhibited. I caught an occasional glimpse of his face as he turned to watch an article of clothing fly and what I saw there was a kind of innocent happiness that belongs to the ancient Trickster soul.

He carefully closed the top drawer and sat back down on the edge of his bed, slapping his fingertips together, just like I had left him.

I made a lot of noise on my way back to the dorm. "I found it, not to worry!" I announced coming down the hall. Standing in front of him, I held out his bathrobe so he could stand, turn, and slip his arms into the sleeves. But he wasn't giving anything away that easily. Remaining seated, gazing off into the distance, he forced me to slip the robe over his back and place his arms in the sleeves for him. Just like always.

I picked up all the clothes, folded them, and replaced them in the dresser as if it were part of the evening routine—all without uttering a word.

Walking Richard back to the living room, I could not help but feel that some veil across the *deep psyche* had been pulled aside for brief minutes, revealing the ancient one living in the secret heart of us all.

FIFTY-ONE
1979

The shaman's rattle called the spirit blessings.

There are three distinct phases to the Corn Harvest Ritual and this was the second: the Vigil, where a small group of extended family members stay awake all night, praying and chanting and dancing. It is a celebration of gratitude for the harvest this year and an appeal for abundance in the coming year.

An open space behind Don Alfredo's house had been cleared and smoothed. In the middle of the clearing a fire leapt, sending sparks to reunite with the stars. To the side of the fire stood the altar: two wooden crosses had been pounded into the ground and then draped with white linen and decorated with bead necklaces. In the moonlight and dancing firelight, they looked like children's ghosts. In front of the crosses stood two huge *ollas*, or clay jugs, filled with fermenting *tesguino* for the next day's celebration.

Around the fire danced the shaman and three women. He danced and chanted and shook his rattle to the sky, shuffling back and forth in a wide arc on one side of the fire while the three women danced and sang, staying precisely opposite him on the other side of the fire. It was as if their dance spaces were bisected by a north-south axis: he danced in the east and the women danced in the west. They never crossed into the other's sacred space. Back and forth, mirroring each others' movements, the dance went on hour after hour. Occasionally, Don Alfredo would carefully approach from the south to add more wood to the fire. The rest of us attending the vigil watched the dancers in the ceremonial space.

Nothing else happened. What else could happen? The air was so thick with sincerity and piousness that there was no room for anything else to enter. There was just that single-pointed concentration of souls that opens the In-Between World to conscious participation.

I lost count of the number of times I *shifted* between the *tonal* and the *nagual* during the vigil. But I never noticed any difference between the two. The dancers' focus opened the *nagual realm* for all in attendance. But it was no different than the dance in the *tonal realm*. Ritual of such long-standing had brought the two realms to the point of absolute identification.

It was like looking at a distant star and realizing you were looking back in time because the light you were seeing was actually emitted thousands of years ago.

The light the dancers were shining was thousands of years old.

FIFTY-TWO
1993

"Movement!" cried the Mixtec *indigene*, dropping the bamboo dice on the table. He moved a green piece along one side of the board, landing on a square occupied by a red piece.

"No!" wailed the German woman. "It was so close!" She picked up her piece and returned it to the home square.

The game had been going on for hours. The rhythm of the dice rolling and the cries of the three players formed an agreeable counterpoint to my codex studies.

"There's no way to stop you, now," the Mestizo musician lamented.

The German woman stared at the board and came to the same conclusion. She shrugged assent.

The Mixtec smiled modestly. "It was so fated," he bowed.

They all stood and stretched.

"It is better to have all four seats occupied," said the Mixtec.

The other two nodded, accepting his word for it—they were the novices and he the teacher. They wandered off to the restaurant on the other side of the curtain for some lunch.

The Mixtec went to the bathroom and then meandered over slowly in my direction, stopping a polite distance and gazing down at the codices opened on my table.

"You can read these?" he eventually asked. He had long black hair and piercing black eyes.

"I'm getting better at it with practice," I replied.

"These are dates, aren't they?" he said, pointing to a couple of panels in the Codex Selden. "This is the Year-Bearer *Rabbit* and this one is the Year-Bearer *Flint*, right?"

"Yes," I replied, "there are four Year-Bearers. *Rabbit, Reed, Flint,* and *House*."

He stared at the codices in silence. "Have you ever heard of the game *Patolli*?" he finally asked.

"I've only seen representations of it in the codices. I don't know any more than that."

"Arturo," he said, extending his hand.

"William," I replied, taking his hand.

"Come look at this, William," he said, beckoning me to follow him over to his table.

In the middle of the table, a large rectangle of amate paper was hand-painted in bright green, yellow, blue and red figures: running around a course of 68 squares, the four Year-Bearers repeated themselves over and over—*Reed, Rabbit, House, Knife, Reed, Rabbit, House, Knife.*

I grunted involuntary surprise.

Arturo smiled appreciatively. "I heard that there was a village in the remote mountains of Veracruz where the old men still played *Patolli* as it was handed down to them from the ancestors. It took me two years to find the village and another year to convince the *patolli warriors* to teach me to play."

"There are too many squares," I thought aloud.

"Yes, but each player runs a course like this," he said, tracing a path with his finger, "so they travel only 52 squares."

I grunted involuntarily again.

"It is a living artifact of the old ones," I said, mesmerized.

"Each of your three pieces is called a *nahualli* and these squares here with the crossed lines are called *nahualli squares,* where your pieces cannot be taken or passed. The other squares are called *tonalli squares,* which can be transformed into *nahualli squares* if you can place two of your pieces on them at the same time."

I had to sit down. The board came alive before my eyes, inducing a euphoric vertigo. The words and images swirled around me like bats from a cave.

Nahualli and *tonalli* are the original Nahuatl words for *nagual* and *tonal*, respectively. There were too many layers shifting back and front for me to get a clear focus. The sacredness of time, marked by the ritual calendar of 52 years. The four directions, marked by their respective colors. The shamanic lifeway, marked by the *nahualli* and *tonalli* squares.

Each of your pieces is your nahualli . . . journeying through a world of tonalli spaces . . . with a few protected nahualli times . . . but there is a technique to transform tonalli moments into nahualli ones . . .

The ramifications were overwhelming. It was a map of . . . what? There was something missing, something I wasn't seeing yet that tied it all together.

"The game is too powerful to be played by human beings," explained Arturo. "It is played by the gods of the four directions. We occupy their seats and they play through us."

"Of course," I said to the game before me.

FIFTY-THREE

1957

"Look at all these books and tell me which one you like the best," said my second-grade teacher.

It was the first week of school and she had moved my desk to the back of the room, next to her own. There was a bookshelf with perhaps fifty large picture books that she wanted me to look through.

Like many of the children in a rural area, I did not come from a family that had books around the house.

I picked up the first book in the bookshelf, took it back to my desk, and looked at each page. I returned it to its place, took the second book to my desk, and looked at every page. It took me several days to look at each page of each book but when I was done I knew which I liked the best.

"Aquatic Dinosaurs?" she said. "This is your favorite? Very well."

She opened a drawer of her desk and took out a huge pad of tracing paper and a box of colored pencils. Setting them on my desk with the book, she said, "I want you to make me this book on aquatic dinosaurs. Copy all the pictures in this book with the colors and words."

I carefully traced every dinosaur from every angle in the book, page by page. I colored them as accurately as I could. I copied every word, including their common and scientific names and the long descriptions of size and habitat. It was a large book and it took me the entire school year to complete. She never moved my desk back and never had me participate in class. She seemed extremely happy when I presented her the completed book.

I always assumed school was going to be like that from then on.

FIFTY-FOUR
2000

"You want a showee?" asked Yoli, the African Grey parrot.

He was just three years old but quick to pick up on patterns—and language.

He'd learned that when I approached his cage with his feeding stand that I was about to ask him, "You want a shower?" And he'd also learned that words could be altered by changing their ending to "ee."

I opened the door to his huge cage and waited for him to climb out on the smaller stand. Instead, he scrambled down to the bottom of the cage, picked up his favorite rubber toy, and clambered back up to his perch. Transferring the toy from beak to claw, he repeated, "You want a showee?" before dropping the toy into his water dish.

I had to laugh as I maneuvered the stand into the cage and got him to climb aboard. I was giving him a shower, so he was giving his toy a shower. It was too cute, I smiled to myself, all the while I held Yoli under the gentle spray of the shower. But I noticed he huddled with his back against the stream of water instead of fluffing up all his feathers to let the water wet his skin.

•

A few days later, I approached Yoli's cage with the stand in hand as I'd done since he was a month old. "You want a showee?" he asked, knowing what was coming. I stopped in front of the cage, expecting him to grab his toy and put it in his water dish again—he, too, was given to patterns.

But to my surprise, he climbed into the water dish himself and began giving himself the most enthusiastic bath imaginable. He dipped down inside to wet his back, he used his feet to splash water up under his wings, he used his wings to splash water on his head, all the while rocking and shaking and nearly dancing in his water dish. Water flew everywhere and Yoli chortled to himself, as happy as I had ever seen him.

After that, I never gave him another shower. Every two or three days he'd ask, "You want a showee?" and then go crazy soaking himself and throwing water far and wide.

The logic of an African Grey is ironclad but not always immediately grasped by us more abstract language-using bipeds. Yoli had tried to tell me that he didn't like the shower anymore, acting out what he wanted by placing the toy in the water dish. When I failed to understand his literal meaning—his language of things-moving-in-space—then he had to actually show me what he wanted.

FIFTY-FIVE
1971

"The *I Ching* is the shortest path to two of the deepest of human desires."

It was one of those monsoons that infrequently strike Southern California and the rain was torrential and unrelenting. It pounded on the roof comfortingly. The courtyard outside was filled with *dancing fairies,* as my grandmother used to call them, where the huge raindrops plopped into standing water.

"You will note," continued Master Khigh, "that I do not say *the only path,* for there are certainly numerous paths, some more direct than others, some more authentic than others, but numerous that lead to these same deep-seated longings. However, there are few paths that lead to *both*. And *none* that do so as directly, authentically and simply."

I had learned that I absorbed his lessons better if I didn't look at him. His face was so expressive that it distracted me terribly. He could not speak more than a few sentences without hinting at a self-mockery that underlay his perception. "Don't you know the story of the master who used to say, *After my first enlightenment, I never stopped laughing?*" he loved to say. I was altogether too serious and he hammered on me constantly to appreciate the vastness of the humor of the universe.

"The first of those deep desires is magic. The longing to participate in the transformation of things is fundamental to human nature. The dream of being at one with the supernatural is part of the waking life of all humanity. The *I Ching* allows every single person in the world to communicate directly with Spirit. Without any training or special knowledge, anyone may consult the Oracle and receive an answer directly from the World Soul. The act of divination, in other words, is magic itself. And the *I Ching*, because it mirrors the very essence of change, allows people to pierce the veil of time in order to anticipate the future and sow the seeds of good fortune. This is high magic, indeed, to be able to participate in the grand process of universal transformation rather than merely being the recipient of fate."

This was a different way of talking about the *I Ching* than I was used to hearing. But now that it was put like this, I recognized that it was just this aspect of the *I Ching* that first drew me to it. I had sensed the sacredness of consulting the Oracle and the sheer magical nature of its reply.

"The second of those deep longings is, of course, enlightenment. Here, too, the *I Ching* provides the most direct path to awakening to the One Mind. As has long been recognized, the mind of the diviner comes to mirror the mind of the Oracle, which encompasses all things and reaches through all times. In particular, it is the quiescent state of the Oracle's mind, before it has received a question, that the diviner quickly comes to emulate. This still point of open awareness, this open potential of Being, that is ever-ready to respond to need—this is the enlightened mind and can be transmitted directly to the diviner through contact with the Oracle."

His words were like dancing fairies on the standing water of my mind.

FIFTY-SIX

1973

"My name is Ray Morningstar and I'm on the Land Trip," exclaimed the short, white-haired, white-bearded, sun-tanned elder. He shook my hand like he was priming a pump. He had the most infectious enthusiasm imaginable.

Ray Morningstar was not his real name. But it was the name he had adopted and he embodied it to the fullest extent imaginable.

"Heaven on Earth is just a deed away," he continued. "And what I mean by that is that we can solve all the world's problems just by everyone in the world signing their deeds over to God. Then no land will belong to anyone and it will all be open to everyone and no one will have to pay for it or pay taxes on it because it'll all belong to God and they can't say that that's impossible because it says right there on their own money, *In God We Trust,* and then there'll be nothing to fight over and war will become obsolete and borders will disappear and there'll just be all these world citizens living together in peace."

He'd been staying at the hotel in San Blas with us for a full minute before launching into his dizzying rant. He ended up staying for a couple of months and spent untold hours with me in the breezeway, rehashing the finer points of the Land Trip.

"Sounds great, Ray," I replied. "But is it legal enough to work?"

"That's what we did up on Morningstar Ranch in Northern California, you heard of Lou Gottlieb, right? Well, we just wouldn't take no for an answer when it came to opening up the land to all comers, so there we found ourselves, in the belly of the beast, deeding the land over to God in the county registrar's office. Man, they did not know how to say *No!*" Ray laughed heartily, slapping his knee.

"Just imagine what it would be like if people could move anywhere they wanted, people mixing together from all parts of this beautiful world, no authority in the world able to say who or what happened on the land anywhere, all the land in the world returned to God's ownership, real *Land of the Free,* you know?"

He could go on like that hour after hour and never missed an opportunity to preach the gospel of the Land Trip to any new guest of the hotel. They might start out thinking they'd been corralled by a madman but after a bit you could see they'd changed a little, *wanting* to share Ray's vision of the potential good right in front of them, just a deed away. Ray wasn't selling anything, after all. He was giving it away.

It didn't matter if the Land Trip was wholly impractical. It didn't matter if the powerful would find a way to turn it to their advantage even if it was legal. It didn't matter if no force in the world could make such a utopian vision a reality.

Ray Morningstar was constructing a paradise, a Heaven on Earth, in the shared imaginal space of the In-Between World. And he was inviting all to the party.

FIFTY-SEVEN
1998

"Have you ever noticed the tendency of Western mystics to use numerology as a means of fixing their intent on real-world goals?" Master Khigh Alx Dhiegh had asked me a quarter-century earlier.

"There were the Freemasons in North America, establishing the U.S. in the summer of 1776. And the Freemasons in Europe founding the Order of the Illuminati on May Day of 1776. And the Freemasons and Rosicrucians of Great Britain founding the Hermetic Order of the Golden Dawn in the Fall of 1887. It makes you appreciate the power of the symbolism of numbers."

It had taken me a minute to see what he was referring to. The 1776 date resolved to 777 when the 1 and 6 were added, just as the 1887 date resolved to 888 when the 1 and 7 were added.

"I won't be here when the next juncture arrives. I leave it in your hands to found something worthy of the miraculous."

•

My thoughts couldn't help but return to that conversation as I prepared the divinatory ritual. Nor could they help but return to the note he had sent me a couple years prior to his death in 1991—

There are no secrets left when the time comes. It is all an Open Secret.

The sun approached its zenith on the Summer Solstice in the magical year of 999 when I began the ritual. Invoking all the great-souled beings throughout eternity to bear witness and add their own intent to ours, I recited the founding dedication I had worked out with Master Khigh all those years before—

In the oneness of time, every moment is a crossroads leading
to every possible present. Here, at this standpoint on this most

auspicious crossroads, I call all the benevolent forces to gather in rededicating the Great Work to a more perfect manifestation of the Universal Civilizing Spirit. To this end, let us hereby expend our collective will to formally initiate the time forthcoming as one of harmonious peace and prospering for all life. As a means to this end, let the Oracle mark this founding with a mandate to forward our highest aspirations.

Taking up the *I Ching* coins, then, I cast hexagram 17 *Guiding Force,* which changed into hexagram 56 *Recapturing Vision.*

I read aloud the key esoteric intent of hexagram 17, *Success comes to those daring enough to initiate a new era,* pausing to allow the words to take form in the air.

After a suitable silence, I turned to hexagram 56 and read aloud its key esoteric intent: *Welling up from its very core, the world of dreaming irrupts into the world of waking.* The words echoed in the still of the Pacific Northwest forest before taking root.

Insects hummed. Birds flitted from tree to tree. A hawk whistled from high overhead. A pair of squirrels chased one another up and down an oak. A light breeze slithered through fir boughs. The crossroads was about to be passed. The compass points were about to change places.

I pricked my finger and drew the two hexagrams with blood on a sheet of *amate* paper. The presence of benevolent spirits was palpable as the forest life around me. Setting fire to the *amate* paper, I watched its smoke rise like prayers into the cloudless sky.

•

It was in this manner that I fulfilled my debt to Master Khigh Alx Dhiegh.

FIFTY-EIGHT

1979

"Today he becomes Rarámuri, doesn't he?" asked Don Alfredo of his father-in-law, Don Rahui. He was using the ancient name of the people before it got misspoken by the Spanish as Tarahumara. The elder shaman nodded once, sharply. He and I looked at each other with the kind of curiosity two museum pieces might regard one another. His face was a rich bronze with creases of experience as deep as the Copper Canyon itself. I was not yet thirty years old and from *the Outside,* a mysterious place beyond the bounds of the Sierra Tarahumara.

The three of us stood in the courtyard of Don Alfredo's house, waiting for his son to arrive with a goat.

There are three distinct phases to the Corn Harvest Ritual and this was the first: the Offering, where a goat is sacrificed to Rayénari, the sun god, and its blood cast to the four directions.

The sun was high overhead in an absolutely clear sky. It was warm for a late autumn day. Little dust devils kicked up along the dirt road leading back into the village. A rooster crowed in the distance and another answered it faintly. Reynaldo trotted up with a goat tethered to a short rope. Handing it over to his father, he withdrew to the house. Don Alfredo led the goat behind the house to the clearing prepared for the Corn Harvest ceremonies.

Don Rahui took up his rattle, removed himself five meters, and, chanting and dancing, began invoking the four directions. Don Alfredo lay the goat on its side and bound its feet with the rope. He placed one hand on the head of the goat, covering its eye, and, looking up to the sun, prayed for the community's offering to be accepted.

Don Rahui approached and handed Don Alfredo a small gourd bowl. Don Alfredo accepted it, bowing his head, and slipped a long, thin knife from its sheath. Don Rahui held the goat's head, singing to it soothingly while Don Alfredo carefully inserted the knife, piercing the goat's jugular and the other side of its neck. Setting the knife aside, he lifted the goat's head a bit and held the gourd beneath the wound, catching the flowing blood. The goat began bleating plaintively.

Don Rahui stood and took the gourd of blood back to his dancing area, where he dipped the rattle into the blood and shook it in the direction of the East. He shuffled to the South and, chanting its invocation, shook more blood from the gourd in that direction. He continued his dance in this way to the West and to the North.

The goat continued bleating. Don Rahui returned to where we were crouched beside the goat and handed the gourd to Don Alfredo. He held the bowl so as to collect more blood and then handed it back to Don Rahui, who repeated his dance in its entirety.

The goat's bleating grew weaker. The sun's rays grew stronger.

Don Rahui returned for more blood and continued his dance invoking the spirits of the four directions.

The goat's bleating grew even weaker. The sun's rays grew even stronger.

Don Rahui's chanting grew louder with every round.

Don Alfredo lifted his face to look at mine. Our gazes locked. I felt the *shift* into the In-Between World like the last number in a combination lock falling into place.

The sun stood still, fixed in place directly overhead. It was no longer "just the sun" I had learned to see as a fiery ball of nuclear fusion. It had an *inside*. Something shining through. Its sole unique being, of soul-making power and life-giving love and delirious light, its awareness, its presence—all this shone through the physical sun: I squatted in the dust beside Don Alfredo, basking in the radiance of the solar deity, who *saw* us and welcomed us into its sight. Ribbons of ochre flowed upward to the sun. The blood, too, had an *inside*: the blood within blood flowed up to be accepted by the sun within the sun. The goat leapt free of its body and Don Rahui stopped dancing and the world stopped turning.

The mountains within the mountains shimmered like butterflies about to burst from their chrysalis. The trees within the trees sighed mists like buffalo breath on a winter morning. Don Alfredo and Don

Rahui were transparent, as well: they were young men, performing the same ritual over and over as years passed into centuries and centuries into millennia. The earth itself had a *nagual body* shuddering and turning and flowering within it—I could see it when I looked down and through my own legs. It seemed to be an egg of immeasurable memory and irrepressible dreams.

Don Rahui walked over to us and crouched down next to Don Alfredo. I had difficulty focusing on him—his *tonal* and *nagual* bodies repeatedly shifted to the fore.

He placed his hand on my right shoulder.

Don Alfredo placed his hand on my left shoulder.

I understood then. The goat was not the only sacrifice. It was the outer symbol of the inner sacrifice—the sacrifice of my blindness to the world as it is.

The cobwebs had been wiped from my eyes.

FIFTY-NINE
1998

Leonor's great-grandmother was a Tarahumara.

•

I was reading a science article.

"It says here that in five billion years the sun is going to die," I said to Leonor.

When she didn't reply, I turned to find her crying.

SIXTY

1973

"How did you become a *curandero*, Don Pancho?" I asked, trying to take his mind off his bruises.

He gently rubbed his black eye. "No one in their right mind wants to be a *curandero*. It is a dreadful responsibility and carries dangers like this."

"But you help so many people."

He smiled tightly, shaking his head. "I know it looks like I am serving others and that I am a good person for helping them but the truth is that I am as mean and petty and selfish as anyone else in the community. There are many of us who wish we did not have this weight on us, who feel that we were tricked into becoming *curanderos* and wish things had gone differently. To you, it looks like I help so many people but to me it is part of a debt that I must repay. Sometimes, like today, I resent it."

I had never seen this side of Don Pancho before. He was always solemn but never morose. He always expressed sympathy for others and never complained about his lot in life. And he had always appeared to take pride in his ability to heal the people who came to him.

"How do you mean you were tricked into becoming a *curandero*?"

A crab sidled onto the concrete breezeway from the beach, stopping a few paces from where we sat. Don Pancho stamped his foot loudly. "What did I tell you last time?" he demanded. The crab reversed its course and disappeared back around the outer wall of the hotel.

"I was a young man like you and I was very strong. I could work all day and drink all night and I had numerous women who were interested in marrying me. I wore a suit and good shoes. I did not dress like a peasant like I do now. I had a job in the city, in a bank, and my prospects were good. Then, one day, for no apparent reason, I became very ill. The doctors could not heal me. I grew weaker and weaker. As a last recourse, I went to the Cora *curandera* in the village where I was born. I did not want to do that because I wanted to be a modern man and she represented the past I was escaping from. But I went to see her, knowing that the alternative was the slow death I was already facing."

He shifted in his chair, trying to get comfortable. He smiled against the pain.

"She told me, 'You have three antagonistic spirits attacking your back and if you do not find a spirit ally soon to protect your back, you will be dead in a matter of weeks.' I did not really believe in such things but I had to go along with her or perish. So I asked what I needed to do and she said, 'Let me feel your neck.' She poked and prodded and squeezed my neck and came to a decision, 'Good, you have a very strong neck. Now, you need to go to the graveyard tonight at midnight and go to the grave of someone who has recently died a sudden death by accident or violence. Then, you must ask that person to become your ally, so that you will have someone protecting your back in the spirit world. But the spirit will not agree unless you make a vow to finish their work in this world.' I really could not believe my ears! It all sounded so much like an old book of fairy tales and witchcraft. All I wanted was some medicine to heal me and here she was, talking about me going on this adventure to the graveyard!"

I frowned sympathetically.

"She was adamant and turned me away, saying that if I did not care enough about my life, then neither did she. I had no choice and so that night I did as she instructed. I wandered around the graveyard looking for signs of a recent burial. I could find only one and so I knelt there, praying for help. All of a sudden, the man's spirit was standing before me, demanding to know what I wanted! I was so shocked, all I could do was repeat what the curandera had told me—I would finish the man's work in this world if he would protect my back in the spirit world. This caused the spirit to weep with relief because it had been so angry and worried about his wife and children. I could not believe it! I was suddenly weeping with relief because I had been so angry and worried about dying so young! In that moment, our spirits made a pact—I had an *ally* and so did he and we would face this ordeal together!"

"How wonderful," I said.

"Yes, my condition began to improve immediately," he replied. "My ally was able to ward off the hostile spirits attacking me and as soon as I was stronger, I went to the house of his family and introduced myself. His wife was naturally cautious, of course, but I explained my concern for her and her children in great detail and assured her that she could ask the curandera about the appropriateness of my intentions. From that time on, I treated his family as my own, making sure they always had food and clothing and the support needed to see his children through school. Other people began to hear about this arrangement and started coming to me for help, thinking I could help them in the spirit world."

He shrugged resignedly. "What else could I do? If I turned them away, they were hurt and angry and turned against me. So back I went to the curandera, asking for her advice. Naturally, she was willing to teach me what she knew if I helped her in return. Well, obviously, taking care of two households that were not even my own took all my time, so the prospects I had had slipped through my fingers and I was set on the path of becoming a *curandero*. She taught me about the plants and rituals of healing and, eventually, about how to acquire other spirit allies who could be sent to help and protect other people who asked for help. In that way, I gained three companion spirits who assist me in the healing work."

"But you still haven't said how you were tricked into it," I reminded him.

"Well, that old curandera was a crafty one," he replied. "She needed an apprentice for her healing work and also to help with her house and *ranchito*. So she had looked around for the best candidate and settled on me. I only learned this later from one of my spirit allies, who explained how she had set those three antagonistic spirits against me in the first place. She knew I would have to seek out her help and then I would be caught in her net."

"She tricked you into being a better person and spending your whole life helping others," I said, unable to keep from smiling.

He laughed. "And I will never forgive the old witch for it."

SIXTY-ONE
1979

"Come help me bring back some firewood," called Don Alfredo.

When I got down to his house, he was shaking kernels of corn loudly in a metal pail. The sound attracted the two horses, who came galloping up from the upland pasture for the treat. While they ate, he slipped ropes around their necks and handed them off to me. I held them there while he arranged the horse collars.

When everything was ready, we backed the horses into place and fitted the yoke to them so that a long pole ran back between them. We secured this in the air with a link of chain and off we went, Don Alfredo guiding them with a long set of two pairs of reins about twenty feet in length.

We headed up the arroyo, keeping to the volcanic bedrock, since there was no trail wide enough for both horses to walk in tandem. The arroyo was extraordinarily beautiful. It was called locally *laja blanca*, white lava, and was obviously the result of an ancient lava flow about five feet deep that cooled with the passage of the flow. This created a U-shaped streambed about fifteen feet wide whose banks were made of the same smooth lava.

There was only a couple inches of water flowing in the stream and the horses were familiar with the way up the arroyo, so we paid little attention to them and spent our time talking about firewood.

"You see that tree over there?" Don Alfredo asked, pointing to a dead pine standing about a hundred feet from the stream. "It died last year, so I'll cut it down next year."

"That tree on the ground over there—I felled it last year, so I'll cut it up for firewood next year."

"Over there, that tree is starting to turn brown. It will almost certainly die in a year or two, so I'll cut it down three years from now."

It went on like that for nearly a half-hour, with Don Alfredo demonstrating an intimacy with his surroundings that I found difficult to imagine. To me, it looked like a forest but to him, it was a carefully stewarded resource, every element of which required utmost consideration.

"And that tree there," he said, pulling the horses to a stop, "I cut it down two years ago, so it is ready for us today."

We climbed up the bank with axes in hand and began limbing the tree. The branches were fairly brittle and so the work went relatively fast. Once all the limbs were trimmed away, I started cutting them into smaller lengths to take back.

Don Alfredo looked up from chopping off the thinnest ten feet of the top of the tree and waved me off. "We'll take this instead," he said, pointing at the tree itself. The plan suddenly took form in my mind and I was startled by its audacity.

Using branches that were stout enough to bear the weight, we pried the forty-foot long tree down off the rocky mountainside and into the streambed. Don Alfredo had me back the horses close enough that he could chain the butt of the tree to the pole running between the team. He tested the tension to make sure the chain was secure. Standing well behind the horses, he took a pair of reins in each hand.

He looked over his left shoulder at me and smiled wickedly. "Ready?" he called as if he knew I wasn't. With that, he slapped the horses sharply with the reins and yelled, "Yah!" at the top of his lungs. The team lunged forward, hooves slipping in the shallow water on the smooth lava. It took a second or two for them to get traction. It took me another second or two to realize what was about to happen.

The team was at full gallop, running downhill, dragging a forty-foot long tree in their wake. The tree was secured at its base, so the lighter end whipped around wildly, not only bouncing up and down, but ricocheting off one rock bank and then the other.

Don Alfredo and I ran side-by-side about mid-way down the length of the tree. He kept whipping the horses to run faster and the tree heaved and wobbled ever more unpredictably, caroming back and forth between the walls of the stream, picking up force with every rebound. Water sprayed off the horses' hooves. Water sprayed off the tree as it swept across the streambed again and again. Water sprayed off our own feet as we tried to keep purchase on the slippery stone.

The rest of the universe disappeared. Nothing existed except what existed in the tunnel of my vision: stream, horses, tree, Don Alfredo. No action existed except those actions that kept me from getting crippled: keeping my balance in the streambed and jumping over the flying tree trunk every time it careened my way.

There was no room anywhere in the universe for attention aimed anywhere else but this long seamless moment of running jumping running jumping running jumping. Completely and utterly focused on the chaotic lurching of the tree, I felt myself *shift* and suddenly moving in slow motion, perfectly synchronized with Don Alfredo, the horses and the tree. What had moments before seemed fraught with danger and desperate timing was transformed into ecstatic dance and buoyant weightlessness. The horses' hooves no longer struck stone, the tree signaled where it was about to be, Don Alfredo floated like a kite at the end of the reins. I leapt and that caused the tree to soar in my direction. Don Alfredo leapt and that caused the tree to soar in his direction.

The universe reappeared. Everything moved together at the speed of sight. Nothing was hidden or outside the vista of spirit. Mountains, clouds, trees, stream, rocks, soil, water, colors, horses, direction, reins, Don Alfredo, chain, tree trunk, me: everything flowed together like kelp in ocean swells. We were in the oneness of time.

Don Alfredo began pulling back on the reins before we got to the end of the arroyo so that the tree's momentum didn't carry it into the horses. As we reached the confluence of the arroyo and the river, he reined the team out of the streambed and up across the field to his house. Time returned to its usual pace. We maneuvered the tree into place and untied it from the horses. We uncoupled the horses and set them back to pasture. We cleaned the horse collars and stored all the equipment. We took our seats in the patio of Don Alfredo's ranchito and watched the sun sink into the canyon lands.

We were still laughing when the stars came out and joined us.

SIXTY-TWO
1993

"Resistance!" cried Tlaloc, god of rain, from his seat in the South. He was blocking the *nahualli* of Chalchihuitlicue from advancing and didn't want to be forced to move his own *nahualli* too soon. "Yes!" he exclaimed when one of the four bamboo dice landed on its edge.

"Bah, you are so lucky," groaned the goddess of water, from her seat in the West. She had maneuvered all three pieces close to her exit square but, instead of being close to winning, was trapped behind South's *nahualli square*.

The dice were passed to Quetzalcoatl, god of wind, seated in the East. He shook them thoughtfully between cupped hands, staring at the board. He whispered into his hands and dropped the four split-bamboo dice, drawing a *five* and two *ones*. He moved each of his three *nahualli* out into the open onto unprotected squares.

"Ah, the act of self-sacrifice," Tezcatlipoca, god of fate, mumbled appreciatively from his seat in the North. He tossed the dice on the table. They all landed face-down.

"Twenty," sighed Chalchihuitlicue resignedly.

Tezcatlipoca advanced his three *nahualli*, capturing all of Quetzalcoatl's pieces and sending them back to start over.

"I'm doomed," sighed Chalchihuitlicue resignedly. By sacrificing his pieces, Quetzalcoatl had maneuvered his *nahualli* behind her. It was just a matter of time until he caught her and forced her to start over again herself.

Since she couldn't move, Chalchihuitlicue passed the dice to Tlaloc, shouting, "Movement!" as she dropped them into his hand.

But the rain god drew another *zero* and held fast, waiting for Quetzalcoatl to arrive.

The game fell into a set rhythm. *Nahualli* pieces advanced, were sacrificed, started over, advanced. Around and around they moved, attempting to complete the grand cycle of fifty-two years and ignite the New Fire of Creation. My own pieces moved with a will of their own. They advanced where they could without resistance but engaged other *nahualli* pieces in ways that I would not ordinarily choose—they captured pieces where I would have chosen no conflict, they sacrificed themselves in order to keep the game going by ensuring another player did not win. There was an impeccability of ethics that held each player to account for the whole of the game. A single lapse of attention could ruin hours of sacred play. And sacred it was, for it reenacted the creation and destruction of each of the four Suns, or four Ages, that gave rise to our own present Age, the Fifth Sun.

It was all laid out there in front of me. The First Sun came to an end when Tezcatlipoca changed into a great jaguar and ate the sun, causing a horrific eclipse—darkness descended as the heavens fell and all humanity was devoured by jaguars. The Second Sun came to an end when Quetzalcoatl took the form of a great hurricane and destroyed humanity by turning the people into monkeys. The Third Sun came to an end when Tlaloc caused a great rain of fire, which buried the people beneath volcanic magma. The Fourth Sun came to an end when Chalchihuitlicue caused a great flood that devastated humanity and turned the people into fishes. We each occupied the seats of the gods whose work led up to the creation of this, the Fifth Sun. We were patolli warriors, assisting in the ongoing creation of the world.

Patoa is the ancient Nahuatl word for *play* and *ollin* is the word for *movement*. These two morphemes were combined to create the word *patolli*, meaning *the play of movement* or *the game of movement*. This furnishes the clue as to the sacred nature of the game, for this, the Fifth Sun, is named the *Ollin Sun*, the *Sun of Movement*. The more that I stared at the board, the deeper I fell into a piercing concentration on the In-Between World of the *nagual*, for here, in the ancient game of patolli, were coded the secrets of shamanic transformation of the *tonal* into the *nagual*. Here, I realized, were the means by which the Huichol couple had pulled me into the *nagual* on the beach in San Blas. And the means by which Don Alfredo had done the same thing so often in the *Barranca del Cobre*. And by which King of the Shadows performed his miracles. And a brujo had pulled Don Pancho into a fight in the *nagual*. Here, in essence, were coded the secrets by which an entire culture had maintained its authentic nature against the forces of colonialism and modernism: long before the Europeans arrived, the Mesoamerican culture of shamanism was establishing a timeless realm of the soul independent of the time-bound events in the *tonal*.

"Tezcatlipoca! Tezcatlipoca!" the other three players called loudly.

"I salute you!" exclaimed Arturo, who had been sitting in the seat in the East.

"I salute you!" exclaimed Anna, who had been sitting in the seat in the West.

"I salute you!" exclaimed Miguel, who had been sitting in the seat in the South.

I returned to the *tonal* and slowly realized I had won the game.

"It was so fated," I replied humbly and meant it.

SIXTY-THREE
1958

You don't need to wake up.

The familiar voice comforted me, lulling me back to sleep. All I wanted was to drift among the clouds, embraced by buoying arms.

You don't need to wake up.

I turned over, trying to find my way back to sleep.

You don't need to wake up.

But for some reason, this rankled. Instead of soothing me, it jarred me awake. I lifted my head off the pillow and looked at the foot of the bed.

Three ghosts, two tall and one short, evaporated into the moonlight.

Then I remembered: I'd seen them before, teaching me while I dreamt.

I laid my head back on the pillow, comforted.

I don't need to wake up.

SIXTY-FOUR
1978

There were no shadows.

A dull red light suffused the inside of the camper. Yet there were no shadows.

I lifted my head a little further off the pillow and looked again, trying to rouse my curiosity.

But a half-familiar lethargy gripped me, pulling me back down into sleep.

You don't need to wake up.

•

Leonor was shaking me by the shoulder.

"Wake up!" she whispered sharply. "There was a red light in the camper!"

I was suddenly fully awake. How much time had gone by?

I leapt out of bed and outdoors in a single movement. I walked around the camper, peering into the night.

Nothing.

We were parked on the highest point in the immediate vicinity. To the South and East lay the Rio Batopilas and the Cascade some fifty feet below the overlook the locals had invited us to call home. To the North and West, the land fell away to Don Alfredo's ranch. There was no one and nothing to be seen.

A thousand thoughts ran through my head. The light had seemed innocuous at first, like the backup lights of a pickup shining through the windows of the camper. Except there were no other vehicles in the village. There were no electric lights since there was no electricity in the village. Though the moon was only half-full, the night was bright enough. There was no one and nothing to be seen.

It was our first night there. We had arrived after a two-day drive along logging roads that inched down and back up the mile-deep Urique Canyon, down and back up the mile-deep Batopilas Canyon, and then back along the ridge for hours before dropping down into the valley that is home to the headwaters of the Rio Batopilas.

We were far away from civilization, perched on the eastern edge of the *Barranca del Cobre*, where the highlands gave way to the winding, twisting canyons running to the sea. There was no reason for our camper to be filled with a red light, in other words. And there certainly was no explanation for how it could fill the camper without casting any shadows.

No explanation.

It sat like a boulder in the middle of a small stream: immovable.

It wasn't a quaint mystery you hear about somewhere. It was a red light suffusing the inside of your camper in the deep hours of the night. Where you and your spouse and three-year old child are sleeping. In the wilderness. Of the Sierra Madre. In Mexico. With no explanation.

It was not the kind of mystery that could be ignored. It could not be moved aside. It could not be reasoned with.

•

The next morning, we made a point of asking folks in the village if they had seen any strange lights. Every single one of them answered the same. Late at night, something flew over the village, following the river from the canyon below. It shone an eerie red light on everything below it and on occasion made a mechanical noise that could be heard across the valley. It had been appearing like that two or three times a week for the past year. Everyone had seen it because it woke them up when the red light went through their homes.

I slept outside the camper every night for the next month, camera beside me, determined to find an explanation. But whatever it was, it never came back in the two years we lived there.

Don Alfredo spoke about it only once:

"The ancient ones told of mysterious sorcerers who derived their power from the left arm of a woman who had died in childbirth. They used that power to enter people's homes at night, place the inhabitants in a strong sleep, and perform all kinds of secret acts upon them."

SIXTY-FIVE
1952

"Do you want to hear a story?" asked the old woman crouched beside her gravestone.

I was born in a cemetery in Columbus, Ohio, on March 16, 1950. There was a hole in the world at that time and people born a few months on either side of that date seem to know what I mean: it was as if everything from the very beginning whispered incessantly, *Walk no one else's road.* There was a hole in the world at that time and the souls who entered then had no one to blame but themselves if they arrived at someone else's destination.

My father was working his way through college and took a job as the caretaker of a cemetery in order to provide for his expectant wife and forthcoming children. My mother and father were poorly matched, fated to spend the next 25 years in high drama before finally calling it quits and accepting the inevitable divorce. The drama had already been in high gear when I was in the womb, so I wasn't surprised by it once I was out among the living. And the dead.

My older brother arrived stillborn. He was buried in that cemetery and, once I could walk, I found my way to his grave by instinct. By that time, he appeared as a full-grown man, so I always assumed that was the form his soul preferred. He accompanied me and my dog, Teddy, on our wanderings among the gravestones, introducing me to the other ghosts and encouraging them to tell their stories.

I was aware from an early age that although visitors came to whisper in hushed tones to the marble headstones, they invariably left without hearing a word of reply. This was a source of confusion at first, since I hadn't yet realized that not everyone could hear the voices of the souls of the deceased.

It was impossible, at that young age, for me to tell the living from the dead. Not that there weren't certain distinctions, of course, like solidity of form and density of voice, but these just seemed like differences of degree and not kind. There were young and old, male and female, happy and sad wherever I looked: it did not occur to me that the living and dead occupied different worlds.

The eldest of my three sisters was born about the time I could walk well and my parents were understandably engaged in taking care of their newborn. This meant that I had free range of the grounds—which came to mean that I was as much raised by the dead as by the living during that time. Certainly, I spent most of my waking hours with them—and, just as certainly, they spoke to me more than the living did.

For my part, I learned not to talk about such things to people as I grew up—until I traveled to other cultures, that is. There, I found that my experiences fell well within the spectrum of normal human contact with the soul.

"Do you want to hear a story?" asked the old woman crouched beside her gravestone.

Her hands were gnarled like tree roots and she wrung them fiercely, as though keeping the next moment at bay. She glanced around nervously, as if fearful that something might overhear her. Her hair was white, her eyes black, and her skin deeply furrowed.

I nodded yes and she began speaking in a singsong voice, moving her hands now in a way that drew pictures in the air, indelibly imprinting their images on my dreaming soul. The dream she painted there in my memory would sound like this if put in words—

There was a terrible dragon made of shadows. With every new shadow, it grew in size and darkness until its wings stretched across the whole world. Everywhere it passed, it brought sorrow and suffering and loss. War and hate and revenge followed in its wake and people everywhere despaired of the life they might have had. But out of the moon, there fell an egg into the sea and when it hatched, a gigantic bird of white light emerged and took to the sky. So enormous was the bird that it immediately devoured the dragon of shadows in a single bite, trailing happiness and good fortune in its wake. People everywhere learned this lesson and from that time on were ever watchful to destroy the dragon eggs within their shadows.

It is true that I was born in a cemetery and had, for the longest time, difficulty telling the living from the dead.

But the last thing I would ever call this world is a *cemetery.*

A *womb,* perhaps. Or a *cradle.*

Or, perhaps most to the point, a *spawning grounds.* A place of return, where souls find their way back to start the journey of discovery over and over.

From the very beginning of this journey of mine, I have had the same lesson demonstrated repeatedly, for what the dead teach is that there is no death.

SIXTY-SIX
2003

Moacir had told me I would see It again.

I was fully awake when my heart stopped beating and my last breath passed my lips.

Without any real warning, a genetic time bomb went off and my body's time came to an end. The moment of death was upon me at age fifty-three and I found it a curious thing indeed. People around me grew quite excited but an untroubled calm came over me, carrying me further and further away from the scene, as if moving me to an invisible but familiar place just sideways to where my body lay. The sirens of the ambulance were soft and melodic, the questions of the emergency room doctors sounded like a different language.

Minutes after they placed me on the emergency room table and fit an oxygen mask over my face, I felt my heart stop beating and I sighed my last breath. At that precise moment, the distinction between my mortal personality and immortal soul became absolutely apparent.

There was the briefest pause while my personality puzzled that I did not gasp for breath nor seem concerned that my body had just died—and then it was lovingly cradled in my soul and I was catapulted, for that is the only word for it, catapulted, wide awake, out of my body and into the Sphere of Universal Communion.

My whole life, it turned out, had been practice for the moment of dying: my soul stepped forward, speaking reassuringly about how it had been through this so many times before. While my personality went mute in the face of the Unknown, my soul catapulted into It with one last sigh of joy and gratitude for this lifetime: *What a glorious Creation!*

•

Moacir had told me I would see It again.

The difference was that this time I was not seeing It from the outside. I was fully awake when I entered the Sphere of Universal Communion.

I do not say that is Its true name or Its only name. I'm not even sure it's possible for it to have one single true name. But the Sphere of Universal Communion is what I saw and what I felt and it's the only true name I can imagine, the only one I can use to describe It at all.

It is a sphere of light, but light that is aware. Not something so much seen—since we have no physical eyes without a body—as sensed. Something like the warmth of sunlight even when your eyes are squeezed shut. But with the additional sense of someone present, close by, their attention resting on the edges of your awareness gently. An aware light that is both the substance and the medium of communion within its own spherical spatiality. An aware light that creates and sustains the possibility of shared awareness on a universal basis. Within its infinite spatiality.

I was fully awake when I realized I was myself a sphere of communion.

A sphere of aware light.

Surrounded by an infinite number of other spheres of aware light.

•

My body was dead for two minutes before the physicians were able to revive me. But for me, months had passed before I was returned to this world.

I can still see It with diamond clarity. The Sphere of Universal Communion appears as an infinite space of aware light that is occupied by all the individual spheres of aware light that ever have or ever will exist. As if it were the One Mind, occupied by all the individual Ideas it ever has or ever will conceive. Or the timeless, dimensionless, Oversoul, occupied by all the individual souls that ever have or ever will enter the realm of time, space, and life. I cannot be certain of Its true name, but of the relation between the Whole and Its parts—and between parts and parts—of this, I am certain.

Each of us, as an individual sphere of communion is the embodiment of two complementary halves: Understanding and Memory. While Understanding is the principal characteristic of our immortal soul, Memory is the principal characteristic of our mortal personality. Understanding is our individual portion of the limitless Knowledge of the One Soul, the evolving insight we possess into the Way of the One, our individual spark of immortality. Memory, on the other hand, is the accumulated impressions of all the lifetimes we recall, the sum of all the personalities we have yoked to our soul, our enduring storehouse of mortal treasures.

Each of us, as an individual sphere of aware light, then, dwells in the Universal Sphere of Communion, a unique fusion of soul and personality, Understanding and Memory. After the death of the body, the soul catapults back to the Universal Sphere of Communion. If it is not yoked to the personality at that time, then it returns without any memory of that lifetime. It has Understanding, perhaps greatly evolved by its experiences of that lifetime, but no direct Memory of it. The personality, likewise, must be yoked to the soul at the moment of dying if its Memory is to accompany it to the Sphere of Universal Communion. Otherwise, it wanders without Understanding, lost and confused among all the other disembodied personalities, unaware that it no longer has a body and is only reliving the Memory of that past lifetime.

As the greatest Teacher of all, Death integrated all the lessons of the other teachers I had been privileged to know during this lifetime. Each, in their own way, had prepared me to meet Death by teaching me to unite the soul and personality during this lifetime, before the moment of dying arrived.

∗

I was fully awake when I realized that whenever another sphere of aware light came into contact with me, there was an immediate and spontaneous exchange between us of our respective Memory and Understanding. When we come into contact, all that we know and all that we are passes uninhibited between us in a natural and open communion of shared being: spheres of aware light touch and exchange the totality of their experience and assimilate one another's experience into their own.

Such moments make clear that all the parts are *reflective* of one another.

∗

I was fully awake when the Sphere of Universal Communion contracted, drawing all the individual spheres of aware light closer and closer, until they all came into contact with one another at the same time. Breaking through every dam of individuality and flooding us all in the totality of our shared being, every individual awareness that ever has existed or ever will exist is spontaneously and immediately At-One with the One. All Memory and Understanding instantaneously passes among all individual spheres. All Memory and Understanding instantaneously becomes One in the synergistic unfolding of the Whole. All Memory and Understanding instantaneously metamorphoses in such contractions as every individual drop of awareness in the ocean of awareness merges into the single sea of communion.

Such moments make clear that all the parts are *relative* to the Whole.

It is impossible to speak about my teachers without acknowledging the profound generosity of the great-souled ones I encountered in the Sphere of Universal Communion. Not only were they kind enough to seek me out and exchange Memory and Understanding in the act of communion, but they held in place long enough to explain and clarify what had been passed to me. Otherwise, what I received was densely packed experience that took time—in many cases, years—to translate into *knowing*. Because of the generosity of such teachers, I was able to leave the Sphere with a much deeper well of knowledge applicable to the world of the living. And, it seems, I left behind those parts of myself that I did not need. A drop of water may fall and disperse into the sea, after all, but retrieving it results in a water drop that does not contain all the original—and does contain parts of the ocean itself.

•

I was fully awake when I returned to this world. As profound the leaving of this world, no less profound the returning.

Between the Sphere of Universal Communion and this world is the realm of the wandering souls, the place where mortal personalities dwell after death, the realm of Memory without Understanding. Here, too, we are individual spheres of aware light. But our light is dimmed here by mortal habits, causing us to relive our life over and over as if we were still alive. Aware only of our Memory of having a body, we wander unaware that we no longer have a body. But the same mechanism of communion still holds true: whenever the mortal souls of our personalities come into contact, all that we are passes between us immediately.

Where the communion with spheres of aware light within the Sphere of Universal Communion was intoxicatingly awe-inspiring, the communion within this realm of wandering souls was disconcertingly heart-rending. This was because contact with those lost souls resulted in their memories pouring into me—and these were universally difficult memories to experience, since they all revolved around unresolved grief, anger, aloneness, shock or fear.

Moving through this realm on the way back to the land of the living, I was overwhelmed by the cumulative suffering that flooded my awareness. It verged on the unbearable—until I realized the full extent of our communion: the sharing between individual spheres did not just flow in one direction. As impacted as I was by what poured into me, those wandering souls with whom I came into contact were many times more impacted by what flowed into them from me. This was so because I had both the Memory and Understanding to place what I was experiencing within the context of the Whole, while they had only Memory of their own lives. The sudden burst of deeper Memory and new Understanding shocked them into full awareness of their position and potential, making it possible for them to cry out to their higher souls and reunite with them in one fell swoop.

This I came to understand as the equivalent of Harry's Rainbow Bridge Ceremony and I continue the practice of journeying to that realm of wandering souls and communing with them, in the hope that they might find comfort in such contact and be able to use what pours into them as a means home.

•

Death the Teacher held one additional lesson for me. Although it is much more difficult to perceive here than in the Sphere of Universal Communion, we are no less spheres of communion here than we are there. Once I had experienced what it feels like to recognize myself as a sphere of aware light in the bodiless state, I had become sensitive enough to perceive myself as that same sphere of communion here with a body.

And sensitive enough to recognize that everyone else is a similar sphere of aware light, as well.

Moreover, although it is even more difficult still to perceive the spontaneous and immediate exchange of Understanding and Memory that occurs when we individual spheres of communion come into contact here, it occurs nonetheless, even if not in our conscious awareness.

I have, in other words, been a wayfarer with a body and been a wayfarer without a body and have not ever found any difference.

AFTERWORD
2014

And now, back to work.

PART TWO
COMMENTARIES

Commentary on the chapters
in Part One

PREAMBLE

The tendency of people to abstract the simple and direct into the complex and convoluted is a side effect of over-reliance on the intellect. All the teachers I have had the honor of learning from took great pains to speak literally. This is because they are speaking about *real things* that are, nonetheless, often imperceptible to the five senses. Communicating about spirit is difficult enough, given the nature of language, and is not clarified by speaking metaphorically.

Real teachings, in my experience, do not rely on abstract reasoning. They are, in fact, dulled and diluted by over-thinking and conceptualization. With that said, however, it has to be admitted that literal teachings about spiritual matters often *sound* metaphorical because words are designed to describe external things and states accessible to everyone's perceptions. For this reason, teachers have to make use of *approximate words* to symbolize concrete spiritual experiences. Students are to be forgiven, therefore, for assuming that their teachers' *approximations* of spiritual experience are merely metaphorical.

The matter is further complicated for serious students by the fact that different teachers rely on different words to describe the same spiritual realities—a fact amply demonstrated in the following chapters, as teachers from different cultures speak about the same spiritual reality, what I would call *The World's Twin*, in different words.

As the accounts in this book demonstrate, by *real teachers* I am referring to individuals who have had firsthand experiences of a spiritual-shamanic nature. I am not referring to religious texts, which by their nature *are* metaphorical.

ONE

To me, he was always Master Khigh and I knew him only as the person teaching me to access the divinatory state of being. I had no idea that he was a successful film and television actor. It was, indeed, ten or fifteen years later that I saw him in his amazing performance in the original *Manchurian Candidate,* where he plays the Chinese brainwashing expert. As an actor, he was known as Khigh Dhiegh and had numerous roles in television, as well. By the time I met him, he had merged his Taoist practice with his art of acting. He took great delight in pointing emphatically to my head and asking, "Who do you think is in there?" After waiting a few dramatic moments, he would drive the point home: "Which of your roles in life have you mistaken for your self?"

Even as the years went by and we remained in contact via mail, he never spoke of his career nor did I ever ask. But this did make a tremendous impact on me as the years passed, helping me resolve the tension between mysticism and practicality in the art of making a living. To see how he took his natural talents and honed them into a way to make a living in order to better pursue his true calling became one of the most valuable lessons he ever gave me.

TWO

Dr. Robert Sharp became a chiropractor so he could manipulate people's bodies in a specific way that he had developed as a means to pushing them into the *nagual.* He termed this method *the press,* which was an accurate description of the bodily mechanics involved. He told me on one occasion that he began his search for such a mechanism while experimenting with another psychic explorer, L. Ron Hubbard, "back before he got crazy with the religion thing." He was a remarkable teacher, not given to talking too much. His perceptions were startlingly clear, in the sense of reading the vitality and sensitivities of people. He could perceive blockages in the body, manifested as a rule in the back and along the spine, and had developed his own mechanics by which to break them up—mechanics that were strangely direct and abrupt and efficient.

His exposure to the concepts of the *nagual* and *tonal* came from his readings of the Castaneda books of the time. He found in those descriptions enough similarities to the state he was accessing that he used them to orient himself and his students within the otherwise supernatural realm. He was particularly adept at instructing and guiding students without interfering with their natural tendencies or directing them according to his own understandings.

THREE

Don Alfredo was the most perfectly adapted human being I have met. He was so utterly attuned to his environment that it was impossible to think it might exist without him. He was like the mountains themselves, utterly solid, completely present, absolutely still. He was already legendary when we met. One of the more well-known stories involved Ysidrio, a younger man than Don Alfredo but just as big and muscular. Ysidrio became ill at that time and Don Alfredo could not heal him with plants and prayers, so he carried him to the nearest hospital some fifty miles away—most of which involved an uphill climb out of the canyon lands. Ysidrio's version of the story merged the heroic with the hilarious, as his illness involved "ugly water," as diarrhea is known colloquially.

Don Alfredo took his time establishing a relationship with me. He naturally assumed that clear-eyed people were wary of one another until some behavior signaled an opening for a deepening alliance. Once we had cleared that hurdle, he was as utterly committed to teaching me as I was to learning. Our bond went even deeper, however, in that Leonor and I became godparents to his son's first child, a daughter they were kind enough to name after my own mother, Laura.

FOUR

Robert was one of the first people to recognize Leonor's innate capacity as a healer. Now, nearly forty years later, she has become a well of healing energy that she shares with all her clients. Not only has she become a masterful body worker but she's a profoundly proficient Traditional

Chinese Medicine practitioner. Robert's encouragement and respect for her open-hearted *being* contributed mightily to Leonor's eventual career.

Such is the behavior of a true teacher, I believe. Neither aloof nor making dependent, a real teacher is, first and foremost, a *real person,* one who engages you with their entire being and does not hold back from entering your family and caring for all concerned. After my tenure as a student with Robert, we kept in touch. He undertook the rather strenuous adventure to find us in the Copper Canyon, where he stayed camping with us for several weeks. He would always say later that this was one of the most memorable journeys of his life. The whole community was prepared for his visit and lined up, day after day, to be healed by the shaman from the North. Since most of the problems folks in the wilderness have are bodily injuries, he was able to alleviate much suffering, all for free, of course, and people talked about him for years afterward. One of the most extraordinary encounters involved a man who brought Robert his horse, hoping he could manipulate the horse's leg back into the hip socket. Robert grew up on a farm and knew the value of a work horse. I watched, fascinated, as he worked for hours trying in vain to work the leg back in. The rancher wept openly with gratitude—and sorrow—when Robert reluctantly gave up.

It was one of the high points of my life to introduce Don Alfredo and Robert Sharp to one another. We sat by the hour, me doing my best to translate between them and them talking more with hands, eyes and drawings in the dirt than with words. Eventually, they got around to working on each other's body and spirit. They both expressed great appreciation for each other's skills and personal power. Likewise, they both later made a point of saying that they had reached accord about the nature of the spirit world and the way it is accessed for healing and creativity. Don Alfredo accompanied us to see Robert off in what was a tearful event for us all.

FIVE

It is difficult to recall today what life was like at that time before cell phones, the internet, or even personal computers. Knowledge was strictly bound to books and there were few truly valuable books about mysticism and divination available then. Likewise, teachers were few and far between in the United States, where one was as likely to run into charlatans as in other countries.

Master Khigh never named his own teacher, although he periodically held rituals to honor him. What he did say, however, was that his teacher was the only adept of the Sudden Enlightenment School of his generation living in the U.S. and that he always considered it his great good fortune to have been his student. Although he would not name other adepts of the School living in the States at the time, Master Khigh lamented the dwindling number worldwide.

I do not disparage the technology that has arisen in the intervening years—I have great hopes for its ability to bring the world's peoples together in a collaborative spirit of grand accomplishments. But its novelty still, I think, seduces our senses and has a tendency to pull us out of ourselves, away from the inner landscape of pure soul. The gravitational pull into a social milieu of disembodied personalities, after all, is not the same as the pull into the spiritual milieu of disembodied souls.

The novelty will wear off and these technologies will become tools and people's attention will return, inevitably, to the greatest teacher of all—Nature.

SIX

There are no adults. There are only bigger children and smaller children. To spend time with creative and open-hearted people reminds us of our own childlike nature, our own sense of unquenchable curiosity, our own capacity to leap into the deep end of life and make it all up as we go along.

Moacir was just such a person. His soul overflowed the bounds of his body. He was music, ecstatic and dancing in place. He embodied the crossroads of music and magic.

It is a crossroads occupied by mystics of many cultures, especially those of Asia Minor that Gurdjieff visited on his travels. It is a crossroads that Gurdjieff himself occupied for many years. To step onto this crossroads is to follow the inaudible into the invisible.

G.I. Gurdjieff was an enlightened master active in Europe and the U.S. in the first half of the twentieth century. His mystical insights were offset by the Sufi-like disdain he held for being treated as a "saint." He went to extraordinary lengths to disabuse his students of the preconceptions of what the enlightened mind looked like, which led to numerous paradoxes in his relationships. For Westerners, unused to this type of teaching method, he was an enigma—rude, abrupt, demanding, arrogant, insulting: a character so off-putting that he could be dismissed out-of-hand. For those who stepped into his presence with an openhearted willingness to learn how to work on themselves, however, he was a charismatic being that could guide them toward their true potential.

SEVEN

I was twenty-one years old at this time and had no money to spend on books nor the background to even know which books I might need to read. Master Khigh was sixty-one years old and had neither of these limitations. He had been studying the *I Ching* for thirty-five years at that point in his life. He held a doctorate in theology and was extremely well-read, with interests extending into comparative religion and psychology. I recognized years later his familiarity with the *Eranos* group of scholars, to which Richard Wilhem contributed, along with the likes of Carl Jung and Henri Corbin. I believe it was the latter that particularly garnered master Khigh's attention, rooted as it was in the esoteric teachings of mystical Sufism with its focus on the primacy of *the Imaginal.* This autonomous realm of pure psyche, what he called the In-Between World, was the focus of what he taught me—how do you enter it, how do you sense it, how do you interpret its images, how do you translate it to others?

Such are the concerns of a diviner, he was convinced, and a large portion of our time together was spent in the pursuit of answering those questions. Compared to the concentration required for that pursuit, the study of the trigrams, hexagrams and line changes of the *I Ching* was relatively easy. With time, however, I came to realize that concentrating on the images of the trigrams and hexagrams was key to the endeavor: it was, as he said, a matter of learning to speak in the language of the Oracle.

EIGHT

How to let go of the body voluntarily. How to slip out of it as if it were a worn-out shirt. How to enter the realm of spirit without fear or distress. How to dispel the illusion that the personality is the soul. How to remain conscious and aware without the body's senses. How to move within the In-Between World without a physical body. How to return to the world of the senses without disorientation or amnesia.

So, yes, what I learned from *the press* was how to move between the *nagual* and the *tonal*—but the real, underlying, learning was at the core level of preparing for the moment of dying.

NINE

The tropical great-horned owl is fearless, the "tiger of the night," the top winged predator of the night. It is highly territorial and the presence of a human being within its hunting grounds deters it little. The haunting calls it was emitting were no doubt territorial, as was its proximity to me in flight. The acrobatics involved in capturing the gecko, turning mid-air, and departing over the obstacle of the railing, breath-taking as they were, must have cost the owl as many calories as it got from consuming the gecko—it is a big, powerful, intimidating creature.

Seeing a dinosaur when looking at a bird allows us to perceive their true nature.

TEN

The original name of the Tarahumara people is *Rarámuri*, usually translated as *fleet of foot*. But it also means *Children of the Sun,* because the sun, too, runs its path across the sky. Their name was distorted to *Tarahumara*, it is said, because the Spanish couldn't hear it correctly and so mispronounced it. They have been, since time immemorial, great long-distance runners. They are members of the same Uto-Aztecan linguistic group that included peoples like the Toltec and Aztec and they remain the only tribe never to sign a peace treaty with the nation of Mexico. They live in the *Barranca del Cobre*, the Copper Canyon, in Northwestern Mexico. Six times the size of the Grand Canyon and deeper in places, the Copper Canyon is carved by two great rivers, the Urique and the Batopilas, which snake through the volcanic mountains of the Sierra Madre Occidental until they reach the lowlands and empty into the sea. It is an incredibly rugged terrain and one that appears on the surface to offer little in the way of human subsistence. It is a testament to the strength of body, character and spirit of the Tarahumara that they not only survive but keep their ancient lifeway intact.

Anyone who has traveled to substantially different cultures is aware of how the very atmosphere of psyche differs palpably from their homeland. Mexico, however, is extraordinary in this sense, as it seems to affect travelers even more so than other lands. Don Alfredo explained this to me once, saying that it was because the ghosts and spirits who had lived on the land still remained, making their presence felt among the living. Mexico was especially strong in this regard, he said, because it sustained such a widespread culture of shamanism—or *nagualismo*, as he called it—to stand against the European colonization. It was this act of defiance that created a reality separate from the one of the colonizers—the *nagual* world where the indigenous soul still lives as always.

This he considered the greatest secret and made it plain that teaching it to an outsider at that time was part of a larger agreement among indigenous people that more and more people needed to be invited into the World's Twin. Only in this way, he was convinced, would people everywhere be able to experience how they *could* live—and how they could carry that world into this one.

ELEVEN

The bats in question would appear to have been Mexican Free-Tail bats, the same as at Carlsbad Caverns. Their numbers are astronomical. Since most visitors to the Copper Canyon see it from above, it is not widely known that the canyons have an abundance of large caves. These no doubt provide shelter and rest for migrating bats.

TWELVE

The Huichol, too, are members of the Uto-Aztecan linguistic group related to the Toltec. They, like the Tarahumara, have retained their cultural autonomy to a degree most other peoples in Mexico have found difficult. Theirs is a culture devoted in large part to the peyote plant, which they hold sacred in living myth and ritual. Like many indigenous peoples, they hold various Pilgrimages to be essential to keeping the life of their people in harmony with the spirit of the land and the sky. The yarn paintings for which they are well-known are remarkable in the degree to which they keep many of the iconic symbols of the pre-Columbian codices alive. Their entire lifeway is a living testament to the power of *nagualism* to make a refuge for the human spirit.

THIRTEEN

There are different kinds of nothing. There is the nothing of pure potentiality out of which everything was created. There is the nothing of mindlessness when the habit mind is stilled and awareness reverts wholly into Being. There is the nothing of the Abyss that haunts the dreams of many.

But there is no nothing like the nothing of an endearing presence suddenly made absent.

FOURTEEN

For the indigenous Ojibwe peoples of south-central Canada, the world is inhabited by many different types of *persons*. Not all those persons are *human persons*. There are *tree persons* and *cloud persons* and *mountain persons* and *deer persons* and *ant persons,* to name only a few. Such a world view permits *human persons* to see all of nature, including themselves, as sacred beings sharing a sacred *world person.*

To my way of thinking, any other kind of perception abstracts the world into concepts in order to maintain emotional distance from the consequences of not acting as a sacred being among all other sacred beings.

FIFTEEN

The In-Between world of the *nagual* is the world of the archetypes, the world of the living messages of the One Mind. We all experience the archetypes differently, evidently, but their forms do not seem to be the point. What message does each give voice to—that seems the focus of the Work. Eventually, however, the focus seems to shift to one's own message. This is the result of our coming to recognize the archetype of our own being—we arrive at the point where we sense the ur-form of our own potential, attuning ourselves to the message of that archetype, whereupon we act forever afterward as an individuated Idea of the universal One Mind.

It is in this sense, it appears, that some people hold close affinity to others, both living and dead. It is because they share the same archetype. They are manifestations of the same angel. The *Messages*, the *Angels*, the *Archetypes*, signify the presence of the various species of manifestations. Each archetype can have multiple embodiments of its message spread across time and place.

It is not dissimilar to the so-called nuclear hexagrams, also called the interlocking trigrams, each of which gives birth to four derived hexagrams. Each of the derived hexagrams comprises the identical interlocking trigrams but retains its individual meaning, nonetheless.

SIXTEEN

Master Khigh later confirmed to me that he was not born *Khigh Alx Dhiegh* but that was his *yang* soul's name as he had heard it pronounced the day it had returned to yoke with his *yin* soul.

The use of formulas, especially those of numerological bearing, to name spiritual presences is not unknown in esoteric traditions. Within the hermetic and cabalistic traditions, all names have a numerological identity as a consequence of their correspondence to their gematria values. It has been oddly reassuring that in recent years I've had the pleasure of meeting several people who spontaneously informed me of their "secret name" or the "name of their higher self." What made these encounters remarkable was the fact that not only did we appear to hold a quintessential sense of purpose in common but that their own esoteric name contained parts or aspects of my own. In those experiences, I had the distinct impression of having met different manifestations of my own archetype.

The most-recognizable of such esoteric names is that of the great beast as named "666" in the Bible's Book of Revelations. This became one of the esoteric names used by Aleister Crowley, a self-proclaimed occultist of the first half of the twentieth century. Crowley remains an enigmatic figure. He was perhaps the first modern person to use notoriety to manipulate the media into making him famous. A talented poet, a master chess player, a world-class mountaineer, and a successful novelist, he preferred to garner widespread fame by drawing attention to his more unconventional proclivities—a self-identified bisexual and drug addict, he shocked the Victorian sense of propriety of the time in order to call attention to his occult efforts to transform the social order. He was initiated into the Hermetic Order of the Golden Dawn by its founder, Samuel Liddel MacGregor Mathers, and traveled extensively to study Hindu and Buddhist practices. One of his minor works, *777*, was dedicated to his "magical son" of the same gematria name.

It is worth noting in passing that some hold that the original spelling of the name Jesus has a gematria value of 888 and stands, therefore, in spiritual opposition to that of the "anti-Christ," 666.

The commonsense person will regard all these matters as of little realistic consequence while those aware of the pre-manifestation realm of the Imaginal will see them as efforts to organize and solidify pure psyche into values and purposes taking root in this world of the five senses.

SEVENTEEN

Like other ancient animist cultures, the lifeway of Australian Aboriginals is embedded in the direct perception of nature imbued with spirit. Likewise, their spiritual tradition of the Dreamtime holds many similarities to the Imaginal realm of other cultures: time is a whole without division into past, present and future; this autonomous universe can be entered by those with the right kind of awareness; and, it is a place of the soul, a place of communing with the living and the dead.

The Dreaming has everything to do with the life of the people, the land and the soul. It encompasses everything from the time of Creation to the ancestral spirits to the sacredness of place and life to the cultural values of the people to death and reincarnation to the individual awareness entering the inner landscape of the Dreamtime while alive in body. The Dreaming carries the very soul of the Aboriginal people, whose continuous culture extends back over fifty thousand years.

The astute reader will have by now recognized an unfolding theme common to the indigenous peoples still holding fast to their animistic worldview: *land and soul are one.* The ramifications of this perspective are profound, for they reveal how love of this glorious creation—the universe, this world, nature, the land, the plants, the animals—places human nature on equal footing with all life and makes of this ever-changing unchanging creation an ecstatic dance of eternal renewal. Not a universe leading to eternal reward or punishment, but a continuum of density of soul, from the most sublime to the most material and all interwoven as a tapestry of ecstatic union.

EIGHTEEN

I believe one must be able to perceive the soul of the land and the soul of the sky and the soul of the plants and the soul of the animals before one is ever permitted to perceive the Anima Mundi, The World Soul, the inner landscape of pure psyche. People who cannot perceive the sacred right in front of their five senses have no hope of perceiving the

Imaginal world. Those who cannot see spirit emanating from all forms within the *tonal* have no chance of entering the *nagual*.

By *soul*, it ought to be understood, is conveyed its analog, *intelligence*. Not the intelligence of reason, necessarily, or human logic, but the *living capacity to be present with the world and learn with the world and change with the world as an integral and intimate part of the world*. Intelligence in this sense is not "thinking" but, rather, *full being*. It is highly emotional, exquisitely physical, and almost entirely directed toward relationships with other elements within its surroundings. Only in a few species, like human beings, is it self-reflective to any appreciable degree.

Animism is mystical union with the One. People who psychologically hold themselves apart from the One, as many modern minds are trained to do, trivialize life, conceptualize death, and desecrate nature. This is the very antithesis of *intelligence*. It is what is formally meant by *ignorance*—to ignore the world as it is, thusness, Oneness. The One, as the Union of the Creative Duality, is Love, and that Love emanates throughout all Creation and guides every being from within. Nature is the great teacher because it is the *embodiment of spirit:* the stars, moon, and sun; the vastness of galaxies within this world of worlds; the minutest of subatomic beings interweaving the tapestry of this world for us; the web of life seeking to explore the fullest potential of diversity; and, the numinous soul speaking from within every form as if each were a burning bush. All is governed by Love and sorrowed are the lives of those who cannot adore and revere the land and its plants and animals and people.

NINETEEN

Superficially, it can be said that one can have comfort and security or one can travel and have meaningful experiences. This is because, too often, comfort and security establish routines that become habits of thought that ignore new experiences and the meaning they bring to the soul. Travel, on the other hand, is not for the timid: there are people and animals and mountains and rivers and weather and all manner of unexpected events to be met and encountered with wonder, respect, and humility. On the other, other hand, however, for the truly open-hearted, all of life, regardless of whether going or staying, is a matter of traveling through this Creation of meaningful experiences.

TWENTY

So many people live in cities now, surrounded by wonderful culture, of course, but deprived of intimacy with nature. This experience of intimacy runs deep. It is analogous, of course, to intimacy among people. But it runs deeper than that, as well, because it establishes the individual's relationship with the One. Ultimately, this is the focus of the soul's work. Intimacy with other souls is the gateway to deeper perceptions, to gaining entry to full and stabilized communion with the Living Whole. In this sense, *intimacy* connotes *a being-with, a belonging-with, an attuned-to,* the One. Intimacy is *a being of one mind.*

Intimacy, too, is a matter of *mutual respect.* If all things are sacred, after all, then so am I. There is no reason one should not be respected in equal degree to the respect one pours forth onto others.

TWENTY-ONE

Most of Don Alfredo's stories were like this one, possessing different levels of teaching about spirit even as they relayed important messages regarding social cohesion. The theme of pride versus humility, in which constancy of friendship proves more consequential than the twists of fate, almost always appeared in some form or another.

Looking at the social and political problems of larger communities, whether urban areas or entire nations, it is plain to see that the lessons of maintaining cohesion among people are fast becoming of the utmost importance. The overarching mechanism by which conflicting interests are resolved in traditional communities involves mediation—it may be that the emerging world culture will govern itself by establishing a *corps of mediators* whose resolutions are considered binding by all parties at each level of society: individual, relationship, local community, regional community, national community, and international community.

TWENTY-TWO

People prone to visions, especially visions of an ecstatic nature, tend to be somewhat taciturn. This is not out of a lack of desire to share what they see but, rather, disappointment in their ability to convey the import of their encounters. This is complicated by the fact that the more sophisticated a civilization thinks itself to be, the more naive ecstatic visions are generally perceived to be. Moreover, the more rational a civilization thinks itself to be, the more such visions are perceived to be figments of the imagination. This is somewhat paradoxical. A *truly* sophisticated civilization stands with mouth agape in awe and eyes overflowing with tears in humility. A *truly* rational civilization recognizes how little it knows and how miraculous the irrational nature of all creation is.

The wise ones among the ancients have long known that concentrating on the ecstatic vision of the world paves the way for it becoming a living reality for the coming generations.

TWENTY-THREE

There is only one thing more difficult than a student finding a real teacher. And that is a teacher finding a real student.

It all seemed so accidental at the time. In retrospect, though, it seems like a well-rehearsed play, its actors moving across the stage and reciting their lines as they have done performance after performance. Who was acting that day, I wondered for a long time. Certainly, my nineteen-year-old personality was overwhelmed by the flow of events and not responding according to past experience. That "I" could not act, having no sense of context or real purpose. It had not even taken the papers in to the meeting, did not even seem to remember that they were the "reason" for the visit. I say "it" because the personality has to be viewed as one-half of the identity and not its sum. There has to be some sense of the "true self" able to view the personality objectively and work to transform it into the most ecstatic expression of creation possible. Without knowing it, my personality was reenacting the age-old pilgrimage of the student visiting the monastery in search of a teacher.

Returning from Arizona, on my way to Mexico, my true self was doing what it had always done—wandering the path aimlessly, allowing destiny and fortune to pull it to the doorstep of a teacher for the personality. I was young enough, my personality still unformed enough, that my true self could come to the fore and act.

For Master Khigh's part, it was all very different. Finding a real student, he could relax.

TWENTY-FOUR

There is a special class of diviner, part spirit-medium and part soul-healer, who undertakes the work of assisting the dead in their passage from the In-Between World to the Sphere of Universal Communion. This is, obviously, an act of high compassion and real devotion. The Rainbow Bridge Ceremony is, to my mind, the least stressful for the practitioner, as it entails little or no intimate contact with the lost souls. Other forms often bring the diviner into close emotional and spiritual proximity with the lasting memories binding the soul to their previous life. Such work ought be undertaken by those who have extinguished every vestige of vanity and self-importance.

TWENTY-FIVE

Our time with Jose convinced me of the inevitability of truly universal suffrage: it is only a matter of time until everyone aged six and above holds the right to vote. Not only is the competence of children vastly unappreciated (principally because it is uncultivated by adults), but their fund of knowledge (regarding issues to be voted on) is the equal of eighteen year-olds. Any arguments against this stance can likewise be marshaled against the ordinary adult.

TWENTY-SIX

Monte Alban was the first great urban center in Mesoamerica, originally built by the Zapotec people and later inherited by the Mixtec. The arts from that center are among the most spectacular from all of ancient Mexico. The Zapotec were extraordinary builders and thinkers. In fact, the oldest inscriptions of the sacred calendar of Mesoamerica are from Zapotec artifacts and not from Olmec, who are the presumed discoverers of the calendar. So important was the 260-day sacred calendar, later inherited by the Maya and adapted to their Long Count mechanism, that the oldest examples of the Mesoamerican writing system are all of calendrical elements.

This calendar was a divinatory instrument, a means to divine the character of someone based on their birth date, or the fortune of a marriage or enterprise, or the nature of things to come. The Mesoamerican writing system arose with its divinatory calendar, just as the ancient Chinese writing system did not arise until the appearance of the Shang divinatory instrument called oracle bones. In these two ancient cultures, then, writing arose as a means to record divinations.

To divine is not dissimilar to practicing *feng shui* or using divining rods to find water, both of which are means of sensing the spirit within the land. The living and the dead overlap at certain moments in certain places because of their mutual reverence for the land. They arrive together at an appointed meeting place and recognize one another according to a prearranged sign. They do not hide but, rather, display their presence with all the elegance and grace of birds of paradise in courtship.

The sacred *Ball Game* was played by nearly all peoples throughout ancient Mesoamerica. It had great cosmological significance, the birth and death of the Sun being acted out on the Ball Court. It plays an important part in the story of the Hero Twins in the Mayan *Popol Vuh.*

TWENTY-SEVEN

Soul *is* images. Images *are* symbols. Symbols *evolve* meanings. Meanings *drive* intent. Intent *transforms* life.

To step into the In-Between World consciously is to encounter oneself as a *dream body* moving among other dream bodies. These other dream bodies may appear as any image at all. This is their power. To act as symbols with transformative potential. This is our power, as well.

Cultivating the dream body is a matter of concentrating attention as if focusing sunlight to a single brilliant point through a magnifying glass. This is accomplished by turning attention back onto itself and not letting it leak out onto inner thoughts or outer objects. *Doubling attention* like this creates an opening into the In-Between World, whereupon we appear to other dream bodies as an image. This image embodies the symbol we have become through the act of *doubling*. This act is not the same thing as self-reflection as we know it in ordinary waking consciousness. But it is analogous. It hints at the mythic property of mirrors and reflections, the stage of identifying one's own *image* in the looking glass.

But in the act of *doubling* we are not perceiving our own image—we *are* our own image.

In so doing, we have reenacted the same creative process whereby the World Soul gave birth to the World's Twin. Creating our own double, we step into the world's double.

On the grand scale, the World Soul is represented by the central circle in Robert's diagram, while the World is on the left and the World's Twin on the right.

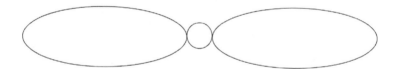

From that original act of creation, the situation has evolved to more closely resemble the third of Robert's diagrams.

On the personal level, intent has the potential to transform life when the dream body maintains its focused concentration on a *meaningful change* that accords with other dream bodies while eliciting no resistance from yet other dream bodies. Intent takes form as image, whose symbolic meaning is perceptible to other dream bodies. It is not wholly dissimilar to fish in the ocean—not only are fish able to perceive other fish, but they can perceive the bubbles other fish discharge. In this analogy, fish are the dream bodies, the bubbles are their intent, and the water of the sea within which all are swimming is the greater dream body of the World's Twin.

TWENTY-EIGHT

Chu Hsi and Shao Yung were important philosophers of China around 1000–1200. They were both lifelong students of the *I Ching* and devoted practitioners of divination. Indeed, Shao Yung is perhaps the greatest *I Ching* diviner to have ever lived and the stories of his predictions survive to this day. He is credited with discovering the Plum Blossom Method of divination as well as transmitting the highly esoteric *Before Heaven Arrangement* of the trigrams. Also called the *hsien-t'ien tu*, this arrangement of the trigrams is said to have been discovered by the great culture hero Fu Hsi, who regenerated humanity 5,000 years ago. Shao was alone among contemporary philosophers in his pursuit of the *Image and Number* school of *I Ching* interpretation. Chu Hsi was instrumental in developing the philosophical school of Neo-Confucianism. His writings on divination are noteworthy for their elegance of thought and subtlety of spirit.

Spirit mediums bringing the messages and wisdom of the great-souled ones out into the open of the present time is little different than the diviner bringing future developments to light in the present. There is also a correlation with meals and the wisdom of the past, as Fu Hsi, the first of the legendary Three Emperors, is linked to food sacrifice. The wu, female spirit mediums, would traditionally participate in important meals of the clan in order to channel advice from the ancestors to their living descendants.

TWENTY-NINE

An acorn that falls on a level plain with loamy soil will grow straight and tall. In five hundred years, it dominates the landscape with its magnificent umbrella of thick branches and lush foliage.

The same acorn, however, that falls into a stony crevice on the ledge of a rimrock cliff will grow gnarled and twisted. In five hundred years, it will be stunted, its branches leaning back away from the abyss and its roots exposed where they grab hold of stone in order to hold the cliff together.

The same acorn.

To my way of thinking, we are not shaped by circumstances. We are shaped by our *responses* to circumstances—by our *relationships* to circumstances. I suppose the personality could be said to make certain decisions about how it chooses to respond to events, especially after it has reached a certain age. But not by the age of nine months. And at any age, really, I think the soul is able to step forward and lead the way toward the most meaningful response. It seems to be a matter of the conscious personality not getting in the way by trying to choose responses based on past experience.

As for the soul, the essence: it is the acorn's drive to survive and produce acorns of its own that establishes its response to its circumstances.

To the acorn that knows nothing of the level plain full of loamy soil, the crevice on the edge of the abyss seems like paradise.

THIRTY

To understand distrust, fear, hatred and violence is easy. To understand unconditional acceptance, universal affinity, mutual respect and reciprocal accommodation is difficult.

When I was born, there were two and a half billion people in the world. At this writing there are seven billion. The psychological stress of overcrowding, diminishing resources, diminishing opportunities and increasing competition exacerbates age-old prejudices and unconscious projections. Stress is largely unconscious, converting into physical symptoms, one of which may be decreased fertility rates. It may not be too long before natural procreation becomes ever more rare and the world population drops dramatically. Our bodies, an intimate part of nature, may be in the process of solving the problem of overpopulation where our conscious minds simply cannot.

But will even that resolve the "distrust of the other" that we have inherited from our ancestors? Will having enough land and resources and opportunities actually eradicate our prejudices and antagonism toward one another?

This was a fourteen-year-old youth who died because of the gulf between people. Had he lived, he would be fifty-nine years old today. Not such a big deal to everyone in a world where people are being killed by the thousands every day, I suppose. Just one more anonymous meaningless death added to the millions of others that have occurred in the meantime, it might be argued.

But he was my teacher.

THIRTY-ONE

I am an advocate for allowing grief to pass through us as fully and unhindered by thought as possible. It is better, I believe, to suffer as profoundly as possible when the wound is still fresh than to try to mete out the pain in tolerable doses. Not only does this permit quicker and fuller healing, but it is also the most honorable way to honor those we have lost.

THIRTY-TWO

What prompts us to act? What causes things to turn out one way instead of another?

We are taught to think of *change* as a symptom or side effect of causality: someone did something and that caused things to change.

But this lifetime has taught me differently: *change* creates causes.

Rather than a side effect of causes, *change* is the environment in which causes arise and fall away. Like the atmosphere of the planet, which provides all the interrelated preconditions to intermix constantly so as to provide the environment in which all the weather phenomena might arise and pass away. Storms and droughts arise and pass away within the atmosphere like causes and effects arise and pass away within the environment of *change*.

Change makes things happen, makes them *fall a certain way*. It is the all-encompassing precipitating factor, imperceptible to the five senses, that prompts actions. Hidden behind the veil of *incipiency*, it blinds any who stare too long into its outpouring of animate intent. *Change is the will of the World Soul and only our souls can sense the rhythm of its tides.*

The soul enters the *nagual*, encounters images in the mirror of *being*, and acts in the *tonal* without falling back on rational thought. The path of good fortune, I earnestly believe, lies in sensitizing ourselves to the living will of the World Soul and allowing our actions to be guided by it: *I am part of a Living Whole that wants the best for me and all others at the same time.*

THIRTY-THREE

The *tesguineria* of the Tarahumara is not dissimilar to the Dionysian rituals of ancient Greece. A several-days long breakdown in the strict self-control required by social and cultural convention, the once-a-year ritual permits the whole self of individuals to find expression otherwise suppressed. Beyond that, the strict adherence to the once-a-year schedule precludes abuse or habituated tolerance of alcohol, allowing for the maximum impact of the "spirits" as a means of achieving an ecstatic state. This is made all the more possible—and socially acceptable—by the ritual's association with religious celebration.

One of the most startling things I have ever witnessed was meeting some of my fellow revelers the day following the *tesguineria*: gone was the grinning, laughing, hugging, joyous, buoyant celebrant of the day before, replaced by the implacable, formal, introverted, polite, standoffish, upright member of the community. I was left with the impression that the entire memory of the celebration was wiped from the person's mind, so utterly different were they. The pressures of sustaining a workable community in the midst of the wilderness take a tremendous toll on the individual's self-expression.

THIRTY-FOUR

Spiritual intoxication takes many forms. But at its core, I believe, is *ecstatic reunion,* a *standing outside oneself,* a voluntary surrender of psychic separateness to immediate at-one-ment with the omnipresent Unity.

In Taoism it is said, "The way of the Tao is return." The going-out of the soul into the physical world is thought of as the World Soul emanating, throwing forward, one of its manifestations into material form. The coming-in of the soul at the death of the body is thought of as its return to the World Soul, an effortless and wholly spontaneous reversion of manifestation to essence. This latter act is accompanied by an almost-unbearable ecstasy. It is for this reason that profound spiritual intoxication, or mystical union in its many forms, is sometimes called *the little death*.

The great Chan master, Lin Chi, once said, "It is the body that awakens." Paradoxically, standing outside oneself shocks the body into the wholly new and unimagined experience of mystical union with the One Mind. Awakening to its own transcendental nature, the body and its younger soul, the personality, are transported by ecstasy into the realm shared by mystics and savants of all Ages.

Shamanic flight is the well-recognized journeying of the soul of the shaman-healer as it ascends and descends the World Axis into the worlds above and below this one.

THIRTY-FIVE

The Tarahumara foot race, or *rarajípari*, covers long distances over rugged terrain. It perpetuates the ancient tradition of the Ball Game as played further south in formal Ball Courts but is restricted only by the distance agreed upon by the teams before setting out. It is not simply a race, however, as it involves maintaining control over the hand-carved wooden ball, about the size of a modern softball, while negotiating trails running along sheer cliffs. Kicking the ball is an art in itself, since the goal is to keep it on the trail. Teams from different villages compete, which involves a lot of status and, oftentimes, gambling in the form of goods or animals. The original name of the Tarahumara, as mentioned before, is Rarámuri, or *fleet-footed*, a signal of how much status is accorded great runners.

Running is a profoundly spiritual enterprise for the Rarámuri. The symbol of *the path* weaves a mystical presence into their lives, a concrete metaphor for the lived life. As Don Alfredo was always reminding me, "To see well is to walk well."

THIRTY-SIX

Canyon de Chelly of northeastern Arizona is a culturally significant place of the Navajo peoples.

The young runner telling us about *the form* also spoke of his great-great-great-great-grandfather as "a five-stone runner," by which was meant that he was able to run up out of the canyon in the time that it took for five large stones to be thrown from the top of the canyon and come to rest at the bottom of the canyon.

Walpi, at First Mesa, is a culturally significant place to the Hopi peoples. It has been continuously occupied for more than a thousand years, occupying a narrow plateau three hundred feet above the surrounding desert of Arizona. It still allows no electricity or running water within its confines.

The Kachina religion is one that ties land and sky together. Like all living religions, its life-creating and life-sustaining forces are not abstract symbols but, rather, dynamic spiritual presences that interact with their human charges in beneficial ways.

The high desert between the Rocky Mountains and the Sierra-Cascades Mountains is home to many of the great indigenous peoples of the Americas. The Inter-Mountain highlands extend south into Mexico, where it is home to the Tarahumara peoples, among others. It is also the historical homeland of the Toltec peoples. The Uto-Aztecan language ties many of these peoples together, from the ancient Puebloans and their Hopi descendants to the contemporary Nahuatl-speaking descendants of the Aztecs.

THIRTY-SEVEN

The swing to the right—not just in the United States but many industrialized nations—in the past four decades is directly attributable to the counterculture movement of the Sixties. So radical—in the sense of tearing out by the roots—was the disruption of the cultural psyche that the right set about to subvert the subversion the counterculture had laid at their doorstep. Certainly, drugs played a part in that uprooting, since their ingestion—especially the psychedelics—offered youth a correlative disruption of the socialization process: new states of mind implied new ways of being, which implied a relatively facile break with the past. The future was wide-open, a new state of mind to be created. The existing order of the status quo had no response to this. They had no idea what the youth were even talking about. Their frame of reference was suddenly obsolete.

Birth control, too, completely took them by surprise. Suddenly women were not solely vehicles of reproduction. Their sexuality was freed up to be enjoyed as much as men's. They could play and enjoy themselves in ways that broke with thousands of years of tradition. The past seemed to be crumbling in front of the standard bearers of Western Civilization.

Nearly free tuition at state colleges and universities opened the door to many thousands of young people being exposed to liberal arts educations that provided contexts for questions pertinent to the day: poverty, war, inequality, injustice, racism, sexism and environmental degradation. Alternative histories, ones that did not paint one's nation in purely glowing terms, shown light on past wrongs and called into question the rightness of the present.

And then there was the draft. The drafting of youth to fight in a war the entire citizenry was coming to question became increasingly untenable. Not just the young people were refusing—their parents could not find the logic or rightness in it. The insubordination and general unsuitability of so many of the draftees was not the worst of it from the elite's point of view—there was the general unrest marked by the anti-war protests.

Massive demonstrations, harking back to the civil rights marches, symbolized the potential for actual *political* revolution. Never mind that the vast majority of demonstrators were simply interested in social revolution, in the sense of a change of obsolete values and solutions to problems—the powers-that-be saw streets full of protestors all across the country and were threatened in a way they had never experienced in the United States before.

The right looked at all this and identified these developments as the problems they needed to solve in order to restore social order. So, the war on drugs and its attendant long-term imprisonment of many thousands. So, the war on reproductive rights, dragging everything from religion to funding into a new objectification of women. So, the skyrocketing costs of higher education, ensuring that we would not again make the mistake of creating an entire generation of well-educated young people from the middle and lower classes. So, the rise of the volunteer army, filled by dangling the carrot of money, education, and housing in front of youth with no prospects for meaningful jobs. And so, the militarization of civil police as a means of suppressing civil disobedience through the threat and use of overpowering force.

The right declared a culture war and set in place a plan by which to right the ship of state. With money, political and religious fervor and unbending self-discipline, they have spent the last forty years trying to undo what was achieved in less than a decade. They have cohesion and a sense of purpose. Theirs is a fight that can be won if the many are unable to find the middle way between freedom and security, privacy and surveillance, and, of course, progressives and conservatives.

The political consequence of Hegelian dialectics is that the few can rule the many if they can divide the many into two extremes incapable of reconciliation.

THIRTY-EIGHT

I am not a contrarian. Far from it. Being against things just for the sake of being contrary is simply argumentative, a sign of intellectual hubris and emotional distance. Nonetheless, I have generally found myself going against the current of contemporary Western culture, much to the enrichment of my life. It is irresponsible to give blanket advice to others about the kind of lives they ought to live, however I do encourage free-thinking individuals to consider alternative lifeways before blindly accepting the one into which they were by accident born. From my perspective, the truly modern person embodies the past generations of all the past cultures.

Having seen the glory of that rainbow on the North Rim, it seems to me that all rainbows are circular, their ends touching underground.

THIRTY-NINE

The Short Path does not depend on cultivation of character to awaken to one's true nature. It recognizes that the awakened mind is *unconditioned*—otherwise it would be limited by causality and, by definition, not enlightened. Being unconditioned, it has no cause that might bring it into being. Because it has no cause, there is nothing a person may do that might bring it about. Therefore, all one *can* do is make a receptive, welcoming, opening in being wherein it might return. In the ancient school this was called, *Making a lodging place for the One.* This is accomplished by quieting habit thoughts, especially preconceptions about the nature of enlightenment. Then, it is simply a matter of waiting expectantly, as if for a loved one that might return at any moment.

Complete wisdom, however, demands that we cultivate character after enlightenment, in order to rid ourselves of conditioned habits of mind that might taint the awakened mind with artificial biases. Likewise, while the Short Path does not depend on cultivation, it does not precisely discourage it prior to enlightenment, so long as it is understood that such cultivation does not result in an awakening but is required in the long run anyway.

FORTY

Fifteen years passed before I became aware of the condition known as *awareness during sleep paralysis,* which could be used to describe my experience. Certainly mine has similarities to others' experiences attributed to ASP. However, for many experiencers, having such an "explanation" (ordinary REM dream sleep is accompanied by paralysis in order that a person does not move and hurt themselves—in ASP, however, a person awakens during sleep paralysis which *universally* results in feelings of terror and the presence of something menacing or evil in the room) does not account for the vividness of the experience. Generally, that vividness is described as many times greater than any other experience, either in waking or dreaming life. Also, it fails to adequately explain why everyone feels terror upon waking during sleep paralysis—many experiencers have these experiences many times during their lives, some with frequency, yet none are able to "normalize" the experience and reduce the terror. The *presence*, too, is unlike any ever encountered in waking or dreaming life. In other words, it is an experience that seems to involve encountering an unknown non-physical, extremely powerful, entity whose intentions are fully conveyed telepathically. There are efforts to explain the condition by applying strong magnetic fields to non-experiencers and producing some of the same symptoms—the problem being, of course, that experiencers are not exposed to strong magnetic fields during ASP. Furthermore, being able to describe how a door is opened in no way describes what it is that walks through that door.

I have had the privilege of sharing this counter-spell of spiritual protection with many others in the intervening decades and have been gratified to see others find it beneficial, as well.

I was not aware of it beforehand, but *exerting intent* is the means of staying somewhere or moving somewhere within the *nagual*. To be clear: this was not something I learned beforehand but remembered spontaneously. It is for this reason that I say such experiences are *tests* or *ordeals* in the old sense of initiations into the next stage of development.

FORTY-ONE

The word *shaman* is not typically used in Mexico, though it has become a bit more common in recent years. A *brujo* is a powerful sorcerer, often the unofficial head of small communities. The feminine form of the word is *bruja*. These are men and women holding knowledge of the sacred technologies of journeying to the higher and lower worlds in order to effect change in this world. This generally means working on the level of soul in order to produce results in the physical world. Much of those efforts are aimed at healing, particularly those that cannot be treated with herbs. Most brujas and brujos are kind, generous, and benevolent people but there are those who fall prey to the seduction of power and self-interest, turning to the casting of curses that bring about illnesses and misfortune.

Curanderos and curanderas, on the other hand, are healers in the traditional sense of using herbs and other physical objects (such as stones and crystals or hot ashes, etc.) to cure ailments. They are considered to occupy a different rung of personal power than the brujos and brujas.

Guilt also played an important part in understanding illness among the Celestial Masters school of Taoism in ancient China. This sect constituted the first *religious* form of Taoism (as opposed to philosophical Taoism). Preventing or remedying illness had to do with various ways in which *qi*, or the vital force, was not leaked, or wasted, through proscribed behavior.

FORTY-TWO

Among the more powerful brujos, there are the most adept sorcerers, called, *naguals*. Their name reflects their otherworldly abilities, such as shape-shifting or magical flight, which are derived from their greater capacity to draw upon the energetic forces within the *nagual realm*. These are oftentimes extremely unpredictable individuals who obey a different set of standards than ordinary human beings. Devoted allies and dreadful enemies, they are given to extremes of conduct.

According to Don Pancho, the relationships between spirits is not essentially different than those between human beings. This is because spirits are motivated by their desires just like the living. By *desires* he meant passions and aspirations making up the spectrum from mystical union and altruistic self-sacrifice to cravings for power and dominance. Understanding the desires of other spirits, while emanating one's own desires as clearly and constantly as possible, makes it possible to forge alliances and accomplish matters here among the living. These alliances were an essential part of his practice as a *curandero*.

FORTY-THREE

The phrase *We Are I Am* pulled back the veil for me, opening the *heart of awareness* to view. The at-one-ment of the universal and the individual, experienced from both perspectives at once in an act of mutual inter-penetration, shone like the summer sun through winter clouds. An unexpected simplicity of interlocking relationships suddenly presented itself for the first time as the foundational symbol of the Unity of the One.

If Death is, indeed, the Great Teacher, what does it teach?

Here are a few lessons I've gleaned from my encounters—

> *Do not trivialize your life*
> *Immortalize every moment*
> *See every being as perfect, enlightened, and mysterious*
> *See everything as sacred*
> *Act as a sacred being among all other sacred beings*
> *Sensitize yourself to the Unchanging*

FORTY-FOUR

The *nagual-pact* is based on the expectation of *mutual benefit*. People operating from within this perception do not view encounters as one-sided: yes, they extend benefit to the other according to the *need* they perceive—but they also expect that the *Great Mystery* has brought them together in order to bestow something of great meaning to them, as well.

Things are happening in the In-Between World that we are not aware of here in the conscious world. Our *nagual bodies* are interacting in ways that we may have no awareness of. We meet in this world yet something much deeper is often occurring in the *nagual* realm. For people like King of the Shadows, there is a symbolic connection between the two realms—follow that symbol and it opens the way to greater good fortune than we can imagine.

There are people who spend so much time in the *nagual* realm that they absorb its power and identify with its intent. Their *nagual body* becomes so strong they can recognize and communicate with the *nagual body* of anyone they meet in this realm. King of the Shadows embodied the kind of respect such people exhibit toward one another.

Moreover, his very presence answered a question it had never before occurred to me ask: *What happens when someone's nagual body is strong enough to enter this realm?*

FORTY-FIVE

Not only was I certain of my goal. I knew with certainty that I was going to find the howler monkey all the way up to the moment of finding something entirely different.

Sometimes you go looking for the monkey but you find the eagle. The monkey would be good enough, of course. It would be great, in fact. But the universe has something better, beyond what we can imagine, if we just commit to throwing ourselves into the *nagual* without reservation.

A couple weeks after leaving Palenque, on my way back to Oregon, I visited a dear friend in Southern California. He had already made arrangements to visit another friend living in a remote area of the Sierra Nevada Mountains and invited me along. The man and his wife had moved a nice trailer onto a plot of land that ran along the rim of a canyon several hundred feet deep. Numerous long fingers of the plateau extended out into the canyon, making walking a little disorienting, since the heavily forested land made it difficult to see too far ahead in any direction. The fellow's wife decided to go for a walk while we were getting to know one another, saying she'd be back in a half-hour or so. About an hour later, her husband grew concerned: dusk was upon us and it would be dangerous walking in the dark—without a flashlight, getting lost was easy and falling off the cliffs a very real possibility. We headed out together to find her, concentrating on the more dangerous part of the rimrock area.

Gradually, we could make out her crying her husband's name. But the geography of the fingers, stretching out into the canyon like archipelagos into the sea, caused her voice to echo unpredictably. All three of us heard the source of her voice coming from different directions, so we split up to better our chances of finding her. I walked more or less directly to her: compared to the rain forest from which I'd just come, the acoustics of the mountains were relatively simplistic.

That experience led me to formulate a kind of double-meaning for every experience: *everything is both perfect in itself and practice for something else.*

FORTY-SIX

There are accidents. There are coincidences. And there are synchronicities. It is essential to treat each appropriately.

Accidents are actual random occurrences that neither mean us ill nor benefit. They are often part of *another person's* life lessons and have nothing intrinsic to do with us, regardless of how they impact us. Another's lapse of attention and hitting us in an intersection, for instance—this is part of that other person's lessons even though it may affect our well-being. That we decide to derive some meaning from it can be problematic: it is as easy to say *This teaches me to forgive* as it is to say *I deserve this for some past wrong.* Accidents are impersonal and attributing meaning to them is not wisdom.

Coincidences are actual intersections of events that carry some lesson of a personal nature. It is among the most direct ways that the universe has of teaching us how to be better adapted, more creative, more compassionate, more cooperative, more patient, more intuitive, more reverent, beings within this glorious Creation. Thinking about an old friend for the first time in years and then bumping into them later that same day is the type of coincidence meant to teach us to honor our intuition—such a lesson often precedes another event where our intuition, if properly attended to, proves especially beneficial.

Synchronicities are especially powerful coincidences that carry profound meaning of a personal nature. A term coined by Carl Jung, synchronicities are *meaningful coincidences* that arise from the *acausal orderedness of the universe.* This last phrase implies that the universe is indeed *ordered* but not in any way that reflects our sense of cause-and-effect. Events coincide without any understandable cause, yet they contain tremendous personal meaning because *they coincide with us, as well.* In other words, the synchronicity is coincidental with the human experiencing it. For instance, as in the story Jung told, a person is recounting a dream in which a golden scarab appeared when, suddenly, a scarab beetle lands on the windowsill with a thud. This is obviously a synchronicity for the person recounting the dream—but it is no less so for the person listening to the dream being recounted.

Synchronicities make a huge impact on people and, in many instances, drive their life-decisions.

FORTY-SEVEN

It was, in some way, similar to my becoming aware of crocodiles earlier that day. Certainly, I *knew about* crocodiles and even salt water crocodiles —had *known about* them for many years. But I had never experienced first-hand the human-to-crocodile relationship as it has existed for millions of years. I had never stood naked and vulnerable before such an overwhelming force of nature. It was the utterly alien and inhuman face of nature that had filled me with that most human of all emotions: awe.

So it was, too, with the meteor. *Knowing about* giant chunks of cold rock flying around in space could in no way prepare me for the utterly alien and inhuman messenger from the universe beyond the Earth. I was awe-struck, staring at the meteor's afterimage for long minutes. Now, no matter where I am standing, I am aware that I stand at the edge of the world, looking out into the vastness of outer space.

FORTY-EIGHT

Because the first enlightened person could not have had any predecessor, then the enlightened nature is intrinsic within every person. Because there could not be any teaching about the awakened true self before the first enlightened person, there is no teaching necessary for any person. Because past, present and future are all one simultaneous continuum, there cannot be more than this single generation of beings. Disembodied awareness is actually embodied space, everywhere present, aware of its own universal nature according to the degree to which beings identify with their individuated forms. For the initiated—that is, the awakened—body, the great matter is not enlightenment but, rather, how to apply enlightened awareness to the historical epoch in which it finds itself.

FORTY-NINE

A shelter home is a crisis intervention facility where children can be brought for the short term while their circumstances can be determined. The primary function is to provide a safe, neutral setting where they essentially have a time out from all the issues surrounding them at the time. Girls and boys aged six months to eighteen years were placed with us for a variety of reasons, the most common of which were child abuse, child neglect, runaway, and nonviolent delinquency. The outcome of their placement was generally divided among: return home to parents; placement with a relative; placement in a foster home; placement in an adoptive home; placement in a treatment center; or, placement in a juvenile correction facility.

Because it stands foursquare at the center of crises, the shelter home intersects with everything touching the children's lives, including: police; social workers; caseworkers; parents, and relatives; defense attorneys; district attorneys; juvenile court officials; probation officers; judges; therapists; physicians; and, school personnel.

Children would stay with us for a couple of hours, a couple of days, a couple of weeks, or a couple of months. We generally had between four and eight children living with us, although there were days we had none and days we had twelve. It was my great honor to share those times of transition with the children in our care.

FIFTY

The owners of the private home for children were in their sixties at the time and had been caring for children with mental disabilities for well over thirty years. While the wife ran the home and supervised the staff, the husband spent all his time working with the children. They were known to the children as *Mister* and *Missus*.

In his own way, Mister had found a Zen mentality of absolutely stripped-down essential interactions that influenced the children in the most positive ways. Although he was constantly paying attention, his gaze never seemed to fall on a specific child. He seldom made eye contact and spoke only when really necessary. Because the home was in a lovely part of Southern California and immersed in the most park-like setting imaginable, the children were outdoors whenever they weren't in the classroom. He would sit for hours while the children played in the fenced-in playground, intervening only when a child's safety required it.

He did not, in other words, *teach*. Not in the sense of giving instruction or telling children what to do or how to do it. If he wanted them to know something, he sat and did it in front of them. Many times. He did not react with frustration. He never spoke down to the children. I was always seeing new ways in which he demonstrated his *respect* for each child—especially, his respect for the child's *capability*. He had made himself into a force of nature, something like wind or rain that wears down stone through sheer repetition.

There was a twelve-year-old girl there with many of the classic signs of autism. She had a short length of clothesline, for instance, upon which were strung some twenty or thirty wooden beads of various shapes and colors. She had the order of this mélange in some perfect, though invisible, order. Woe to us all when one of the other children rearranged the beads on that string—she would wail at the top of her voice for hours, completely inconsolable. Eventually she would tire and take up the desperate work of placing them back in their ordained order.

She loved to swim and would appear unexpectedly in her swimsuit. Approaching Mister, she would point at the swimming pool, and say "Ah-ma."

"No, say *mama*," he answered neutrally, looking out across the playground.

"Ah-ma," she would repeat.

"No, say *mama*," he would answer.

This might go back and forth three or four times—but no more. If she didn't say it right, he would just shake his head and say, "Go get dressed."

What struck me about these encounters was their ritualistic nature. Neither seemed to have a personal involvement. Maybe it was a test of wills. Or it was just some special attention the girl wanted. But when denied the pool, she didn't throw a tantrum or cry or even pout. She just went back and got dressed again.

If it was a game to her, she understood it wasn't a game to him: he wasn't going to stand around and repeat himself forever. If she wanted to go swimming, she would have to relent and say *mama* pretty quickly. And that is just what she did on two occasions that I saw. After one or two *Ah-ma* tries, she said *mama* clear as a bell.

"Okay," said Mister neutrally and into the pool she would go. There was not any sense of winning or losing or of teaching and learning—not in the ordinary sense, at any rate. The lessons, as I watched them delivered over time, had to do with the wearing away of learned habits—he was simply more stubborn than the children and they respected that. He met them on their own ground and, over time, got them to meet him on his ground. These lessons served me well in subsequent years working first, with children in the shelter home and, second, with students of my own.

After I had been working for Mister and Missus for several months, I learned that their own son had been born mentally disabled and that they had raised him well into adulthood, when he could no longer be cared for at home.

FIFTY-ONE

The male shaman danced in the eastern hemisphere of the circle, while his female counterparts danced in the western hemisphere. In accord with the most ancient traditions of Mesoamerica, the West is considered the direction of women. Likewise, important marriages recorded in the pre-Columbian codices are shown as having occurred in years associated with the West.

The collective concentration of attention within a group of people, especially when accompanied by rhythmic song, music, drumming or dance, has long been used as a proven method of opening the gate to the In-Between World. Participating in ancient indigenous rituals is like time travel: not only does it transport one's spirit back to a time closer to Creation, but it carries one's soul back to the very Creation of the World itself.

FIFTY-TWO

Arturo was kind enough to make me a copy of the Patolli board on amate paper before I left. I hesitate reproducing that without his consent, so below is the reconstruction of the board that my collaborator, Martha Ramirez-Oropeza and I worked out. The artwork around the board is from the Borgia Codex. The squares of the board are all precisely the same as received from Arturo.

Artwork by permission, Martha Ramirez-Oropeza

The four Year-Bearers can be seen in the corners of the board, moving counterclockwise from the top-right: Reed, Flint, House and Rabbit. As can be seen, the same four day-signs repeat every four squares on the playing board.

FIFTY-THREE

Real teachers, in any field, are difficult to find. Those who work with children have an especially important part to play in the way that youngsters view learning. The argument can be made, I believe, that the movement toward standardized educational measures, well-intentioned as it is, is ill-conceived and counterproductive to real learning. Individualized instruction is certainly more difficult and places greater importance on the role of the teacher, but the focus on *what* students are to learn will only pull them further away from learning *how* to learn. A side effect of such an approach is that it deadens curiosity and initiative, turning the excitement of learning into one long series of exercises in rote memorization.

This turns schools into instruments of social conditioning and teachers into children's first exposure to conformity police. The noble profession of teacher, so honored in most cultures, suffers by the stress placed on maintaining control of student behavior. Once the trust in teachers' capacity to assess students and individualize instruction has been removed, then they become mere functionaries dispensing officially-condoned knowledge. This differs little from birds feeding their young predigested pabulum.

The blatant nature of such an educational system is not hidden from students' view. The lack of respect for their true capacity, manifested as channeling them through the shearing chute of conformity, turns students into resistant learners and behavior problems. So, the entire enterprise is counterproductive, in that it creates the very lack of conformity it seeks to implement.

Real teachers inspire a love of learning. Real educational systems inspire teachers to greatness. Real communities strive to nurture the potential of their every child. Real societies are made up of free-thinkers.

FIFTY-FOUR

The African Grey parrot is generally cited as the most intelligent creature on Earth, next to human beings. Their intelligence is demonstrated in their ability to *use* language, not simply mimic it. Their memory, likewise, is extraordinary, as good as a person's, despite having a physical brain many times smaller. They are highly emotional, leading people who live with them to say that it's like living with a three-year-old child forever. Which is a long time, when you consider they have a lifespan of *at least* eighty years. African Greys are routinely passed to two or three generations of family members.

We raised Yoli for nine years from the time when he was one month old. The first months were like having an infant, requiring he be fed every several hours. We never tried to teach him to talk—he just picked it up by listening. Being flock animals, their social bonding drives them to mirror other members of the flock. It was a great privilege to share our home for so long with such a magical creature. When we sold our house in the country and began traveling more, we were extremely fortunate to find a loving family wanting to adopt Yoli.

FIFTY-FIVE

The twin quests for magic and enlightenment—such are the ancient dreams calling diviners back into a more original mode of being.

The idea that all of life can be explained rationally falls flat once people experience the extraordinary life within the Imaginal. Likewise, the idea that human consciousness is restricted to the sum of the body's experiences falls flat once people experience mystical union with the One Mind.

The Imaginal, as the realm of living archetypes, opens the gate to the magical presence of original psyche: universal psyche is unconditioned soul in its formless aspect prior to being constrained by the conscious and unconscious forms of an individual. To reenter this state of the *co-conscious pre-individual* (to use a term advanced by Gerald Heard) is to step back into the ancestral memory of all life and, ultimately, all matter.

Enlightenment, as the awakening of the true self intrinsic to every being, opens the gate to the unchanging presence of original mind: universal awareness is unconditioned idea in its timeless aspect prior to being constrained by the birth and death of an individual. To return to this state of the *co-conscious post-individual* (a corollary term advanced by Heard) is to step back into the quintessential understanding of the relationships between all change in all times.

The *I Ching* bridges the gulf between the World Soul and the One Mind: suspended above the abyss between psyche and awareness, the Oracle's gaze pierces the three times of past, present, and future, while the Oracle's voice penetrates the illusion of separateness.

During the two years I studied with Master Khigh Alx Dhiegh, much of his instruction to me revolved around meditation and concentration on the hexagrams and trigrams. This he felt was instrumental to sensitizing ourselves to the Oracle, which he held as the "speaking" of the World Soul (an emanation or manifestation of the One Mind). The starting point was with the trigrams, which he taught were our "real senses," those that we can use to sense the underlying reality of the world of appearances. "Mountain is the archetype of all things holding still," he would say. Meditating on this trigram meant finding that sense within ourselves and thus being able to recognize all the manifestations of the archetype of holding still, wherever they appeared. The *presence* of Mountain was the object of such meditations. Because there is not "inside or outside" in the non-dual universe, Mountain is a presence of me as much as anything else. Obviously, this is so for the other trigrams. Meditations on the hexagrams focused on the interaction of the trigrams, which he felt was more essential than grasping the hexagram as a whole—this, because the hexagrams have taken on interpretations based on cultural perceptions and historical events, whereas the trigrams are living archetypes of natural phenomena. It was not that he discounted the hexagram commentaries, to be clear, but that he felt meditating on the trigram interaction revealed the deeper essential meaning of the hexagram that lies beneath the cultural-historical artifact. "The only difference between people is their sensitivity to the One," he always maintained—and that it was the Inner Work of diviners to make themselves ever more sensitive to the One whose speaking is, literally, the Oracle.

Being first and foremost a Taoist, Master Khigh distinguished between meditations and concentrations. The first meditation was of course one of mindlessness in which there are no objects of thought but a return to essential Being. This has analogs in Chan/Zen, especially as represented in teachings like *The Secret of the Golden Flower.* The second type of meditation, described above, was an identification with the trigrams and hexagrams. Both these meditations were accompanied by breathing exercises he had learned from his teacher—

1. Counting: Inhale, counting to 4; Hold breath in, count 4; Exhale, counting to 4; Hold breath out, count 4.

   Same, increasing to count of 6 each.

   Same, increasing to count of 8 each.

   The point is to reach a very slow rhythmic breathing that no longer relies on counting.

2. Inhale: Breathe in the hexagram (visualizing its lines) from the Oracle.

   Hold breath in: Visualize the hexagram as its trigrams.

   Exhale: Breathe the hexagram back out into the Oracle (speaking back to it in its own language).

   Hold breath out: Empty the mind/imagination in preparation for breathing in the next hexagram.

3. This focused attention/concentration opens possibility to access altered state of awareness.

   Marked by "womb breathing," which is essentially breathing so slight it is imperceptible, creating the sense of breathing through one's umbilical cord, connected to Heaven and Earth.

The use of ritual objects, especially a candle, were held to be valuable but, again, being a Taoist, were not held essential: formlessness of form, the need to be able to perform one's meditations without external forms, was held to be the ultimate form. But ritual actions and objects, he taught, were valuable because they sacralized the meditation, which through personal repetition, fused with the meditations of other practitioners throughout the ages in a collective return to the Act of Creation. This return has implications in that it opens a way for the divine to be in more direct contact with the Oracle—by reentering the sacred space of Communion, diviners make themselves more open to the World Soul (and its voice, the Oracle). He likened this to Jung's idea of the Collective Unconscious, to the Sufi idea of the Secret Garden, and even to the Dreamtime of the Australian Aborigines. Concentration, or as he called it, single-pointed concentration, was key to entering this sacred space. He was aware that there were other divinatory instruments, other sacred technologies, endemic to other cultures and he felt that the indigenous Taoists shared the animistic-shamanic worldview with many of them.

The concentration exercises focused on some straight-forward ones, like clearing the mind and then concentrating on the question in a way he called *driving a wedge into empty space.* By single-minded concentration, sometimes for 30 or 60 minutes, he believed the diviner's mind achieves a deeper rapport with the Oracle. Certainly, I feel this is so, having benefited from those exercises. The more complex one was what he called the *4,096 Exercise*, which consisted of (over a long period of time: it took me months) visualizing every hexagram turning into every other hexagram through a specific formula of line changes. It was "4,096" because that is the square of 64 (including the 64 hexagrams that have no line changes).

FIFTY-SIX

Personally, I never gave Ray's rants much serious attention. They appeared untenable and fraught with possible unintended consequences. But I did take Ray seriously. Here was someone so absolutely devoted to an ideal—an ideal, it must be pointed out, that could not possibly bring him any personal gain—that he would dedicate years of his life to spreading its message. Ray had, by changing his name to the name of the commune where the experiment was carried out in vain, *become* the message. He had made of himself an archetype and ceased living in the ordinary world for the most part. He lived in the Imaginal, he looked out at the world from the Imaginal, he spoke from the Imaginal. He had become an ecstatic: he stood outside himself. He was enthused: he was possessed by a god. From where he stood, he was acting for the benefit of all, he wished only the best for all.

Enthusiasm is contagious. Conviction is compelling. But those two elements still do not move people to change without the third, binding, component: absolute altruism.

FIFTY-SEVEN

The In-Between World of the Imaginal contains the pre-manifestation substance still in the process of taking form in the world of the five senses. Shamans journey within the different realms of that world in order to bring back change in this world. Devout religious people strive to enter into that realm of divine presence in order to pray for change in this world. Dervishes dance themselves into an ecstatic trance by which they gain entry and effect change in this world. Diviners bring their full concentration to bear on a question in order to be welcomed into the Mind of Heaven and return with understanding of developing change. The means differ superficially but the *Work of Change* is essentially the same among the initiated everywhere: first, concentrate attention in order to enter the Imaginal and, second, concentrate intention in order to shape pre-manifestation substance into an archetype to take form within this world of the five senses.

FIFTY-EIGHT

The tree within the tree is the *angel of trees* within the tree. The mountain within the mountain is the *essence of mountains* within the mountain. The blood within blood is the *eternal archetype of blood* within blood and the sun within the sun is the *soul of the sun* within the sun.

The world within the world is the World's Twin shining through the world of the five senses. The body within the body is the *dreaming body* within the physical body, the *nagual* within the *tonal*.

FIFTY-NINE

I stand speechless before the unspeakable.

SIXTY

There is a tendency among many spiritual healers and teachers to talk in what I think of as *opposite speak*. It is a way of speaking that is essentially self-deprecating or pokes fun at other healers or teachers. The reason, I believe, is an effort for the community of healers and teachers to eschew vanity by pulling themselves down off any pedestal others might place them on. This tendency, too, can be seen in other indigenous traditions, such as Taoism, Chan, and Sufism. There is, for example, the case of a teacher and student walking along and coming across a funeral procession. The student pointed to the coffin and asked the teacher, "Is he alive or dead?" The teacher replied, "I will not say, I will not say!" The student pressed the matter, saying, "If you don't say, I'll strike you." The teacher replied, "It doesn't matter—I will not say." The issue at hand, I think, is the unwillingness of the initiated to speak about things in a way that could create a backlash in the Imaginal realm. For the initiated, words are themselves angels, direct and immediate messengers of *spiritual intent*. They are not spoken here in the *tonal* but, rather, in the *nagual* and so carry the weight of the momentous.

The underlying moral of Don Pancho's story was that he was wasting his life and natural skills in the pursuit of meaningless activities and that the village healer recognized this and set about maneuvering him into becoming a healer himself and fulfilling his true potential. His story is fraught with absurdities in order to deflect from the courageous act he undertook in the cemetery acquiring allies, as well as the long practice of apprenticing to the curandera. He "blames" the spirit helpers for telling him that she was the one who set the antagonistic spirits against him—this is his way of deflecting the *responsibility* he accepted for changing his life. Likewise, his story about working in a bank and wearing a suit—this is his way of criticizing the lifeway of those who have lost touch with the land and become something they truly are not.

SIXTY-ONE

The first time Leonor and I hiked up from the Urique River at the bottom of the *Barranca del Cobre*, we met a rancher living on the rim of the canyon. A small, wiry cowboy of mixed European and Tarahumara blood, Donato proved eager to show us some of the points of interest of his land. The most notable was a balancing rock that overhung the canyon floor some six thousand feet below. It was a huge stone, twenty-five feet long, ten feet wide and six feet thick. It must have weighed at least half a ton. It was worn away underneath in such a manner that the point where it balanced on the rock beneath it was only two feet across. Donato clambered up on the shorter, thicker side of the stone that overhung the land and motioned for me to climb out on the longer, thinner side that overhung the abyss. Once we were in place, he began rocking the stone up and down, calling to me to help. Together, we managed to get the balancing rock of Divisadero to teeter-totter up and down several feet. It was perhaps the most reckless thing I have ever done. But something happens to the spirit when the body is most fully alive. It enters a timeless place of spiritual intoxication, an ecstatic trance, that spans lifetimes, binding them with the knot of a newly-created *transcendental memory*. Stringing these memories together through repeated association is like stringing pearls on a necklace, the circularity of which embodies the immortality of the true self.

SIXTY-TWO

Among initiates, there is a perspective from which all of Creation is a Sacred Game and all of human experience is Sacred Play. This reasoning rests on the fact that there are definite rules that souls must follow while they have a body. This resembles the circumstances of a person playing an ordinary game: the rest of the world at large ceases to exist, in a sense, so long as one is immersed in the rules of the game being played—and that the person "returns" to the real world once the game is ended.

Many games have an esoteric side to them that is not immediately apparent to those playing the exoteric, literal description of the game.

These esoteric versions constitute a microcosmic sacred game reflective of the greater Sacred Game of Creation. They have a ritualistic aspect that essentially serves the same function as religious ritual: the return of the participants to the Act of Creation.

SIXTY-THREE

I believe this is a more common occurrence than people generally recognize. The dead have a vested interest in the living. They worked all their lives toward some goals and with some purpose—oftentimes without consciously knowing what those were specifically. After their death, many things become clearer and their hopes of seeing their goals accomplished and reaching closure are strong enough to motivate them to try to communicate with the living. The sense of purpose is often less specific and more universal in nature—again, that may be clearer after death than while alive. Purpose has more to do with abstract relations, values, priorities, perspectives, and intentions—matters that are best expressed through the teaching of ideas and sharing of experience.

Many people are visited nightly by spirits seeking to encourage benevolence: they speak from the experience of their own mistakes while living, aware in death of the consequences of self-interest, envy, selfishness, distrust, and fear. For many, this constitutes a large part of their sleeping life—they have long convoluted conversations with the spirits that are nonetheless forgotten the next day.

The episode I have recounted here was notable in that it was the first time I awoke during a teaching session and in that moment I could remember all the other times. Up to that moment, those other episodes had been completely forgotten, as though they comprised an entirely different half of my life. Obviously, this state corresponds to the In-Between World of the Imaginal realm—the difference being that it is the concentrated focus of the dead that breaks through into the world of the living in order to effect change here.

SIXTY-FOUR

The first and greatest of all the *nagual*-sorcerers was Tezcatlipoca, whose name is rendered *Smoking Mirror*. The "smoking mirror" was a reference to obsidian, from which mirrors were fashioned—as well as arrow and spear points. It is also a reference to the moon, which appears as a "smoking mirror" as it moves through its phases in the night sky. Likewise, it may also refer to the pupil of the eye, the epitome of a "smoking mirror." It is the nature of Tezcatlipoca to move fluidly among identities like this. One of the primary identification markers is the smoking mirror that replaces the foot he lost in a battle with the Earth Monster in an earlier Age.

He was the ancient Mesoamerican trickster god of fate, the shape-shifter responsible for the sacrifice of Quetzalcoatl and his subsequent metamorphosis into the Morning Star, Venus. There is an archetypal representation of him in the *Fejérváry-Mayer Codex*, where he is portrayed with *the severed left arm of a woman who died in childbirth* (this is a provocative symbol, as "women who died in childbirth" were held in the highest esteem and considered great warriors who had died in the battle to bring new life into the world). The arm in question is held

Artwork by permission, Martha Ramirez-Oropeza

in such a pose that its hand covers his mouth, signifying, perhaps, his keeping the secrets of sorcery. That depiction is also remarkable in that the 260 days of the sacred calendar are shown associated with specific parts of his body and accoutrements, an indication of his mastery of the cycles of time.

As the prototypal *nagual*-sorcerer, Tezcatlipoca embodies the two-fold nature of adversary-protector. He put human beings through great hardship, yet the outcome of those trials perpetuated an evolutionary transformation that carried individuals and society forward. The shape-shifter aspect of the *nagual* was well-recognized, chronicled in ancient portrayals as half-man, half-animal protecting the community or its fields. With the Spanish conquest, the adversarial aspect of the sorcerer became exaggerated and associated, inevitably, with the devil.

Pre-Columbian Figurine of Shaman Changing into a Jaguar

Don Alfredo was intimately familiar with the *nagual*-sorcerers in the Sierra. But he did not associate them with these strange lights flying over the village. Instead, he related "the lights" to the ancient pre-Columbian stories of sorcerers who entered homes and performed dark acts on the inhabitants by causing them to fall into a deep sleep from which they could not awake. From this, I inferred that he had heard stories from members of the community about such "visitations"—or had experienced them himself. It also seems to imply that such visitations have been part of the oral tradition of Mexico for centuries.

I have tended to follow Don Alfredo's example of neutrality in this matter. There is ample evidence to say that *something* utterly extraordinary and inexplicable has occurred. But there is not enough evidence to say exactly *what* it is that has occurred. The connection between unidentifiable lights, somnambulistic torpor, overpowering visitors, and the *nagual* remains an intriguing but as-yet unproven one. Should there prove to be such a connection, it may prefigure a collective exploration of the *nagual* as the In-Between World opening onto worlds the existence of which the modern mind has yet to envision.

The dual nature of the experience played out a couple years later when, upon returning to Oregon, I unexpectedly began seeing the *I Ching* as composed of heretofore undiscovered mathematical operations. This was unexpected in the sense that I had never had any special interest in mathematics, let alone in what seemed at first an unnecessarily esoteric form of binary mathematics. That discovery and subsequent decades of research led eventually to the publication of my *I Ching Mathematics: The Science of Change.* So, as troubling and mysterious as the experience was, it somehow awoke a dormant capacity that allowed me to advance the art of divination into the next generation.

SIXTY-FIVE

I find no kinship with traditions that value the spiritual over nature or that denigrate the material world as an inferior creation. I cannot attune myself to traditions that hold this world as evil or that one's existence here is the result of past wrongdoing. I am a stranger to traditions that do not hold this world sacred.

As I understand it, this world—which is to say, of course, this universe—is Our Creation. It is the material emanation of Our Collective Intent. In its natural form, it is a miracle of Perfection, a perfect reflection of Our Vision of Underlying Harmony. Its social form, however, is still in the process of perfecting itself. This is the result of the "physical endowment" of the body—its instincts, in particular, but also its desires and aversions. Our attempt to make matter fully conscious and not merely alive means that there is a sustained process of metamorphosis that the collective body of civilization must complete. The shadow side of the individual is the microcosm of civilization's collective shadow. Our Collective Intent is still muddied at the level of individual intent and understanding. Those driven by the physical endowment possess stronger shadows and more specific intents—they also tend to band together based on shared aversions, which manifests in a civilization of violence, greed, intolerance, fear and desecration of nature.

The grandeur and wonder of Our Creation will achieve full Perfection when the vast majority of souls forge a single alliance of Light, Light and Love that eradicates the prevailing shadow as instantaneously and easily as turning on a light removes all the dark from a room.

In this sense, it is instructive to recall that, while darkness is merely the absence of light, light is not the absence of darkness—it requires energy (intent) to radiate light.

SIXTY-SIX

In the year following my experience with death, I wrote of the understanding I had gained from that encounter, especially in terms of preparing for the moment of dying:

> *Those of us who have died and come back know that it is not the body that is alive—at the moment of dying, we slip off the body much as we slip off comfortable clothes. Because it never was alive, the body cannot die.*

What is really alive is like a wind, or breath, of clear and color-less light—an immaterial form of living awareness penetrating the lifeless form of matter. Because it lives before and after all matter, the immaterial spirit cannot die.

The marriage of spirit and matter gives rise to a child that iden-tifies with the body—a material form of living awareness tied to the body much as a flower's perfume is tied to the soil. Because it is the offspring of two deathless parents, the material spirit cannot die. Those of us who have died and come back know that nothing dies.

Writing from the soul's perspective like this, I found that I had to confront numerous perceptions my personality had long held true. That was particularly so of assumptions regarding "life" and "identity." What appears to be living from the perspective of the personality, in other words, appears to have been a vehicle for life from the perspective of the soul. The same is true regarding what I think of as me. Where social conditioning teaches me to identify with my personality, the death experience teaches me to identify with my soul.

One thing I have found in common with others who have been touched by death: we return with a sense of purpose—we don't know what that purpose is, but we know immediately when we step off the path that leads to it.

CONCLUSION

Robert Sharp used to say that I was born to be a diviner. His logic, as he often repeated it to me, was that—

> *animism was the first religion,*
> *shamans were the first priests,*
> *diviners were the first shamans,*
> *spirit mediums were the first diviners.*

My earliest experiences provided me intimacy with the spirit world and gave me the impetus to search out the kinds of places and people that could deepen my participation in that world.

I look back on those first years and try to remember how I saw the world before I understood it. I do know that it took me a while to understand that the visitors who came to the cemetery were not just headstones that could come and go as they pleased. Odd as this sounds today, it hints at the reason I've had trouble telling the living from the dead: from the very beginning, I have heard the voices of souls speaking, not just from the grave but from within the living, as well.

And they have not ever sounded any different to my ear.

Because the soul speaks independently of the living—and often in a surprisingly different voice than that of their personality—the entire world is filled with the song of souls moving between lives, a secret garden of sheer mountains and lush valleys and dancing rivers flying toward moon-inspired seas. It is a bright timeless dream, crystalized within the In-Between World—the kind of dream that exists once one knows anything of immortality.

I bring up immortality because the dead see the living as twofold beings—one, the personality that's convinced it is the sum of the body's experiences and, the other, the immortal soul moving from body to body, lifetime to lifetime. Of course, the dead see themselves the same way: if they still haunt this world, it is because they have not yet stopped identifying with their body's personality and remembered their immortal self.

So I have learned to listen with two ears: even as I keep one ear attuned to the voice of the personality, I keep the other attuned to the voice of the soul.

And they have very seldom sounded the same.

To repeat: all my life, I have heard the voices of souls speaking, not just from the grave but from within the living, as well.

What exactly have I heard?

First and foremost, it is the souls of the living sighing for freedom from the constraints of society that the personality has accepted.

Even as the personality speaks of the love, acceptance, recognition, and success offered by social conformity, the soul speaks of meaningful purpose, lifelong allies, endless discovery, and collaboration on the widest scale. Even as the personality speaks the language of self-interest and self-importance, the soul speaks the language of benefiting the whole and the sacredness of everything. Even as the personality speaks of wrong roads and dead ends, the soul speaks of homecoming and metamorphosis.

So I have learned to listen to the personality and the soul at the same time.

And I have rarely heard them echoing one another.

As it turns out, there are so very few individuals whose personality and soul speak the same language. Just as I once watched people whisper to gravestones without hearing the soul's reply, I have watched all my life as people talk to themselves without hearing their soul's reply. Mistaking the personality for their true self, they so occupy their attention with the personality's habitual thoughts, feelings, and memories that there is no room left for the soul's gentle call to seek peace and well-being for all.

I have also heard the souls of the dead sighing for freedom—freedom from the compulsive memories of their last lifetime. Because the personality is the sum of the body's experiences, it cannot conceive of the bodiless immortality of the soul. Although the soul hears everything the personality says, most personalities go their whole life without ever hearing the pure song of light continually pouring forth from the soul. Taught about the soul in church or books, the personality imagines what it might feel like to experience it and so interacts with its preconceptions rather than its actual soul.

Sadly, this failed communion then persists after the death of the body. Even as the personality recounts the memories of its body's experiences, the soul recounts its understanding of the perennial truth. Even as the personality laments the loss of its bodily sensations, the soul laments its inability to influence the living more profoundly. Even as the personality relives its past lifetime as though still alive, the soul relives its deathless communion with all other souls.

I have learned, in other words, that nothing is as uncommon as a conscientious communion of personality and soul. Nor is anything as important. All that we come into contact with reminds us that it is impossible to fully experience each moment without their shared presence.

AFTERIMAGE

The diviner is a hollow bone,
the primordial flute,
through which the divine wind,
the speaking,
of the Oracle passes.

It is with profound joy that I place this volume in your hands. In doing so, I would like to recount one last story. It was in 1985, in the magnificent ruins of the ancient Mayan city of Palenque. We had left San Blas and had been in Palenque for over a month, spending our time in the ruins and the surrounding jungle. Leonor and some other folks went into the museum there on the grounds and I decided to stay outside and wait for them. I took up a bench in the shade and allowed my attention to flow out into the sounds of the midday rain forest. It is the constant drone of insects, I think, that disrupts habitual thought and pulls us out of ourselves into the lushness of the teeming forest. The insects were very loud that afternoon, rising and falling in pitch as if intimating something momentous near at hand. An elderly couple sitting on a bench across the courtyard stared at me, trying to make eye contact. They conferred between themselves, came to a decision, rose from their bench and walked directly over to me. They stood so close, I could not rise to greet them.

"Are you the one we are supposed to meet?" asked the woman, bending slightly so as to be able to be heard by me alone. They were in their eighties, dressed in traditional indigenous clothing that I did not immediately recognize. But their demeanor I recognized—it was identical to the elderly Huichol couple I had encountered in San Blas just a couple months before.

"You are on a pilgrimage," I observed, not really intending it to serve as a reply.

They nodded and the woman took my hands and pressed them close, shaping them into a cup. At the same time, the man formed a similar cup with his hands and tilted them forward directly above my own hands.

Letting go of my hands, the woman spoke in a low, singsong voice. "We pour our lives into yours," she recited formally in Spanish. Whereupon the man began chanting in their native tongue as he gazed into the space between our cupped hands. It was a tongue I had never heard before, with complex rhythms and tonal inflections, marked by clicks and whistles. Like the woman had, he pitched his voice so that no one outside our circle could hear him. His voice blended into the drone of the rain forest's insects.

I was no longer sitting in the courtyard outside the museum in Palenque. I was in the Sierra, a rugged landscape as always, but a lush cloud forest instead of high desert. Images flew by of the village and its fields, young people laughing, the cathedral, holy days, effigies and shrines, dancing and music, childbirth and death, strangers and illness, and animals, always animals and plants, always plants. It was a whirlwind, a mosaic, of emotions and memories. It bore the earmarks of great joy and profound nostalgia, both. It was a recounting of fears and courage, youthful hope and aged acceptance, tradition and the passing away of tradition. It was an act of nobility. Of honoring the life given.

Abruptly, the chanting ended and the couple looked at me, directly meeting my gaze. I could feel the tie about to break, I was about to return to Palenque. I was old, standing next to my lifelong companion, looking down on a young stranger possessed of our memories. I was young, filled to overflowing with feelings and perceptions I was remembering for the first time. I was awakened to the oneness of time by the simple act of open-hearted communion.

They smiled with their eyes. And blinked. We were back in the tonal.

The man pulled his cupped hands back to his chest and I did the same reflexively. To speak, I knew instinctively, would have muddied the waters. They turned and departed with obvious relief, the purpose of their pilgrimage fulfilled. And the purpose of my own pilgrimage expanded anew.

·

So it is that I pour my life out into your hands with similar relief. The lessons I have been graced with should not disappear with me—I am humbled and grateful to have lived long enough to commit them to writing.

It has been my intention in this recounting to be like the moon—to reflect the light of my teachers. After all, when teachers pour their understanding into you, it is with the expectation that you will pass it on to the next generation in turn.

There is something more to it than that, however. Something deeper and more meaningful. The act of passing on teachings, when performed by a true teacher, is the very embodiment of care, concern, and love. The student fortunate enough to meet such a teacher finds herself or himself embraced in a subtle loving-kindness, a heartfelt concern for his or her true self. It is one of the keys by which the outer master awakens the inner master.

In that vein, it is my sincerest hope that I have not just passed on information to you—but that the loving-kindness bestowed on me has likewise found its destination in your heart.